Pastor Wendy Berth
call, listening for Goc ....g ways to help
others understand and live his call. This book provides a
biblically based, thorough explanation of the path to a life
within God's call.

—Steven A. Harr,
founding partner of Munsch Hardt Kopf & Harr, P.C.,
co-founder of Call Inc.

Not since Clarence Stoughton's *Whatever you Do* from over
a generation ago, have I seen a more helpful, down-to-earth
guide on Christian vocation. *Custom Designed* is concrete,
helpful, and biblically based. There is no more important
question than the one the book asks: "How do we live worthy of Christ in our daily lives?"

—Dr. Walter Sundberg,
professor of Church History, Luther Seminary

Everyone wants to feel unique. Everyone wants to feel spe-
cial. The good news, no, the great news, is that you are! In
Custom Designed, Pastor Wendy Berthelsen helps us explore
our giftings and the giftings of those in our homes, our
churches, and our workplaces. She makes abundantly clear
the biblical truth that we are wonderfully made for a divine
purpose! There has been a lot of confusion over spiritual gifts
and natural talents. *Custom Designed* helps to bring clarity
and integration to gifts, talents, skills, and calling. As the
leader of a very large organization, I have learned that we all
have unique strengths and weaknesses, gifts and talents, and
that we can be of most use to the Kingdom of God and hap-

piest in our life when we bring these all into alignment. You have a custom designed life—find it and live it!

—David A. Dahlin,
executive vice president, Compassion International

Few church members seem to grasp that God has a calling on their life, that the Spirit has gifted them to fulfill their ministry, or that this is not only for just those in paid ministry. Wendy Berthelsen makes a compelling case that each believer is designed and equipped for a unique calling. Think of the transformational power of church life as these truths are discovered and lived out! Having known Wendy Berthelsen for a long time as her pastor and friend, I have been impressed with her exemplary life, faith, creativity, and ministry.

—Dr. Morris Vaagenes,
senior pastor emeritus, North Heights Lutheran Church

custom
designed

custom designed

A Life Worthy of the Call

Wendy A.W. Berthelsen

TATE PUBLISHING & *Enterprises*

Scripture quotations marked "NAS" are taken from the *New American Standard Bible* ®, Copyright © 1960, 1962, 1963, 1968, 1971, 1972, 1973, 1975, 1977, 1995 by The Lockman Foundation. Used by permission. All rights reserved.

Scripture quotations marked "NIV" are taken from the *Holy Bible, New International Version* ®, Copyright © 1973, 1978, 1984 by International Bible Society. Used by permission of Zondervan Publishing House. All rights reserved.

Scripture quotations marked "NRSV" are taken from *The Holy Bible: New Revised Standard Version* / Division of Christian Education of the National Council of Churches of Christ in the United States of America, Nashville: Thomas Nelson Publishers, Copyright © 1989. Used by permission. All rights reserved.

This book is designed to provide accurate and authoritative information with regard to the subject matter covered. This information is given with the understanding that neither the author nor Tate Publishing, LLC is engaged in rendering legal, professional advice. Since the details of your situation are fact dependent, you should additionally seek the services of a competent professional.

The opinions expressed by the author are not necessarily those of Tate Publishing, LLC.

Published by Tate Publishing & Enterprises, LLC
127 E. Trade Center Terrace | Mustang, Oklahoma 73064 USA
1.888.361.9473 | www.tatepublishing.com

Tate Publishing is committed to excellence in the publishing industry. The company reflects the philosophy established by the founders, based on Psalm 68:11,
"The Lord gave the word and great was the company of those who published it."

Book design copyright © 2009 by Tate Publishing, LLC. All rights reserved.
Cover design by Tyler Evans
Interior design by Nathan Harmony

Published in the United States of America

ISBN: 978-1-60696-969-4
1. Religion: Christian Life: Spiritual Growth
2. Religion: Christian Life: Personal Growth
09.05.18

Dedication

Joel
My very best friend, number one
encourager, and "cheerleader."

Amara, Stefan, Philip, Ana
I'm so proud of you!

Acknowledgements

I am very grateful to these friends and family who knowingly or unknowingly contributed significantly to the message of this book, or prayed during its creation.

Mary Bauer
Cindy Berg
Joel, Amara, Stefan, Philip and Ana Berthelsen
John and Marilyn Berthelsen
Julie Brandsness
Becky Burnison
David and Kari Dahlin
Edsel and Beverly Dureus
Mary Edwards
Angela Faulkner
LeRoy and Val Flagstad
Richard Foster

Steve and Kathy Harr
Harriette and Bob Hedderick
Hope Lutheran Church
Linda Kesti
Dan Knudsen
Tammy, Keith and David Liansi
Kathy and Ed Longstreet
Rollie Martinson
Liz Moulin
Watchman Nee
Todd Nichol
Greg and RaeJean Noschese
Naomi Palmquist
Brenda and Jim Rogers
Lowell Satre
Connie and Jeanne Sorensen
South Range Lutheran Parish
Ken Stokes
Walter Sundberg
Steve, Toni, Naomi, Daniel and Jonathon Thorson
Jim Upton
Morris Vaagenes
Fred and Gloria Wiebusch
Suzanne Wiebusch

Table of Contents

Foreword

A generation ago, the great Roman Catholic theologian Karl Rahner (1904–1984) had this to say about what he called "the theology of the future":

> *The theology of the future will, in a more direct sense than hitherto, be a missionary ... theology ... For in the future the church will no longer be held up by traditions that are unquestioningly accepted in secular society, or regarded as an integral element of that society. The community church will be transformed into a Church made up of those who believe as a matter of personal conviction and individual decision.* (Theological Investigations, *tr. David Bourke [New York: Seabury, 1975] 40)*

What Rahner said thirty years ago has come to pass. Increasingly, to be a Christian is to make a decision to become a Christian. One can no longer depend on Christendom to carry the faith across generations by custom and habit. This is especially true in American society. We live in a country where religion is privatized as a constitutional matter. Our forbears had experienced the dangers of religious coercion from the state and religious warfare among competing churches and fled to this new land to be free. To separate the church from the state was a good thing. To be sure, ours was a society steeped in the Christian tradition and so the impact of all things Christian in the public square remained strong well into the twentieth century. But in recent years, Supreme Court decisions enforcing the separation of church and state, secularization of education, culture and media, and religious diversity among new immigrants have had the effect of reducing the social effect of Christian faith.

The only way to proceed, it seems to me, is to embrace the privatization of faith and turn it to a divine purpose. We have to know as individuals what it means to be a Christian; how God seeks to lead us in our daily lives; what his purpose for our lives is. St. Peter tells us: "Always be prepared to make a defense to any one who calls you to account for the hope that is in you, yet do it with gentleness and reverence..." (1 Peter 3:15). To be prepared to give account of ourselves may be the most important responsibility we have as Christians. Only if we know why we are Christians can we witness to others about the glory of Christ.

To this end, Pastor Wendy Berthelsen has prepared a helpful and clear guide. *Custom Designed* is a superb resource to inventory one's life in light of God's Word and to discern the hand of God at work in the choices we make and the paths we follow. We are not here by accident. We are called into the gift of life by the Creator and sustained by his caring love. Every person has a purpose and a destiny. Our lives are meant to be worthy of the gift we have received. *Custom Designed* can change your life.

—Dr. Walter Sundberg,
professor of Church History,
Luther Seminary

Introduction

Custom Designed
Custom Called

Before age thirty, I had already co-authored and even presented pioneering research at an international symposium in Europe. As a research engineer at the largest biomedical technology company in the world, I was awaiting the awarding of my third US Patent as well. People were impressed with my bright future in the cardiac pacing industry. Though much of my job was first-rate, sorry to say it, I was often bored. Tremendous colleagues, excellent pay, remarkable opportunities, the best kind of boss, measured prestige, a progressive environment—these were all mine. Nevertheless, if windows had been in my cubicle, I would have been found focusing out there. Most definitely, God had called me to that place for a time, but deep down restlessness kept pushing me towards transition. Now for over twenty years, I have been helping people to hear God's call through transition after transition. It's been nothing short of an adventure for me. For you, it will be the same. Do not be afraid.

Transitioning through twists and turns, I have been a daughter, sister, friend, student, neighbor, wife, missionary, mom, volunteer, visionary leader, author, teacher, workshop facilitator, and pastor, among still other things as well. Many meaningful stops have marked the way, and wonderful companions have accompanied me. Over and around our globe, up and down, my Lord has walked steadfastly alongside of me. My God is calling me to more yet to be discovered. Maybe this does not sound the least bit exciting or inviting to you. That's okay! My adventure will not be your adventure. My call will not be your call. God's call is custom designed for you. Profound meaning and purposeful destinations await you.

A bit of insecurity and fear—does the mere mention of "God's call" evoke these feelings within you? If it helps at all, you are not alone! Keep going—it's merely a hazard along the way. My God is not the author of fear.

For quite some time, I have felt called to write this book. There are several reasons why I feel a bit insecure and fearful. First, there was a time when I really never thought of myself as an author at all. After all, authors are those who have already published books. I suppose a second reason is that I wondered if I would ever become a published author. In this age of publishers and consumerism, I know that I am not famous or even a highly sought-after speaker, as are many authors. When I began writing this manuscript, I did not even have a formal paid position. I did not have the right kind of credentials for anyone to pay serious attention. I have even observed this to be the case in conversations with other peers and colleagues. Though I had an outline for the ensuing chapters, I did not know quite how to begin, nor did I have a title. I wondered, *When completed, will anyone want to read it?*

However the plain truth is that I do feel "called" by God to write this book; in fact, I feel compelled. I share these insecurities and fears because God calls people who feel inadequate to the task, people who perhaps have no recognized credentials, people who come from small places and are short on confidence, people who are insecure and have little audience, and people who are aware of their shortcomings, failures, and weaknesses. Of course, God calls the opposite kind of people as well: people who are overconfident and who think that they do not have many shortcomings, failures, or weaknesses. God calls all of these people to do great things. All things that God calls us to do are great things—even if they appear small.

Your insecurities and fears may differ from mine. We will navigate around and through some very common insecurities and fears. By identifying and confronting these insecurities, I am hopeful that they will diminish and even be left in the distance. Because God knows how easily we all become afraid, over and over again God says to each of us, "Do not be afraid." If you are called to something, I have come to know that God will richly provide and graciously give you everything that you need to do it.

To address a common misunderstanding, over and over again it must be said that God does not call just people in the Bible or pastors or foreign missionaries or professional church staff, but God is calling everyone—and more specifically and importantly, God is calling *you*. God's call to you does not necessarily mean that you will eventually become one of these people, nor are any of these higher callings. God calls and needs all kinds of people.

Who am I?

What am I to do?

Perhaps you are seeking answers for these two questions. Though these questions are quite practical, they are also big questions with eternal significance. They are life-defining and fundamental. Maybe you feel one or the other lurking somewhere beneath the surface.

On the road, for a long period of time, I lacked answers to these key questions. Feeling directionless, I first became somewhat aware of these questions while in college. I could master the sciences. So, well-meaning people prodded me to pursue them. In reality, I mastered many fields of study, but no one ever asked me, "Where do you find joy or meaning? What connects with your other unique points of interest?" Feeling uneasy, I shifted from science to math to business and back again to science, searching for a response to:

What am I to do?

Initially unknown to me, the first inquiry was related to a second:

Who am I?

Still, there was yet another query:

How and where do I find the answers?

I was confident of God's hand upon my life. Even though I did not have a roadmap or compass for my quest, some-how I knew that God was walking with me along the path. Looking back, my Lord was moving me ahead and calling me, even though I knew little about God's call to all people. My Lord was leading me.

God's call is not static and unchanging, but very dynamic with many transitions. Perhaps you find yourself in the midst of transition. You may be approaching the end of high school. You might be looking ahead to college, or a trade, or a job or the military. You may be stationed at college or maybe you are just departing from college. Maybe you are newly married, or you have recently become a mom or dad. Maybe you are in your forties and feeling distracted by some kind of restlessness or, even worse, job burnout. It could be that you are trying to navigate some kind of life-changing event— such as the death of someone near and dear, a divorce, or sudden unemployment. Maybe you have recently been set free from some kind of addiction. Perhaps you are anticipating retirement, or maybe retirement feels like a dead end. My mom is a healthy, smart, and financially independent woman in her late seventies who recently experienced the death of my dad. His death left her with all kinds of time on her hands, asking, *What am I to do next?* Until your very last day, God will still be calling you.

Perhaps you are wondering how God's call connects with these two big questions:

Who am I?

What am I to do?

In fact, the first may surprise you. God's call shapes and forms both your "being" and your "doing." So, who are you? You are God's unique child! Though simple, this insight is really deep and profound. As a child of God, you are not a clone of another. Rather, you have all the uniqueness that you received when you were born to your earthly parents. You are custom designed with unique gifts, talents, experience, personality, and much more. God knows every detail of your unique individuality.

Then, what are you to do? Because you are custom designed by God, what you are to do is also custom designed for you. Miraculously, God has uniquely created, crafted, prepared, and gifted you for all that you are to do. Actually, God's call has to do with all those unique places and destinations where you find yourself day by day: your work or school, family, friends, church, neighborhood, community, and world.

When your "doing" is based upon who God has custom designed, created and called you to be, you will actually enjoy (have inner joy) what you are doing and where you are going. God will give you a deep sense of meaning and fulfillment—quite the opposite of what some people might expect. Furthermore, though you may work and work and be physically exhausted, quite surprisingly, you will walk away energized, motivated, and even excited to do more of the same. Along the way, you will still experience hazards— frustrations, roadblocks, hardship, and suffering. But even in the midst of these trials, God will guide and call you. God's Spirit will sustain and empower you; and as a result, you will be *serving* God and others. So, do not be afraid!

God will personally lead you, offering direction to you through the life-giving words of Scripture. Because I have received practical insight and wisdom from the words of Scripture, I once explored nearly every "call" passage. As you seek and search, these sacred words will guide you, imparting time-tested wisdom to aid you as you trek along. Some of this wisdom may be immediately valuable to you, and some may not—at least not right now. While discovering the fullness of God's call, you will also uncover the answers to those two life-defining questions.

Ask God to speak to you through his Word. Ask God to guide you, using your thoughts, desires, and emotions. Ask God to navigate with you through and around any fear, leading you on an amazing adventure. When *fear* appears and creeps into your being, bear in mind that God is not the author of fear. "Do not be afraid." Beware, fear can detour you. Ask God to give you inner courage. Remember, God's call is custom designed for you. Inner joy, peace, fulfillment, meaning, and significance will mark your steps as you travel and traverse over many a path of God's magnificent plan.

"For surely I know the plans I have for you, says the LORD, plans for your welfare and not for harm, to give you a future with hope" (Jeremiah 29:11, NRSV).

God Is Calling You!

God's call may seem like a mystery to you. Who am I? What am I to do? Do you struggle to answer these two questions? One or the other of these hurdles may plague you.

1. You may be just plain *busy* living life–propelled along from one hour to the next by all that you have to do.

2. You may *not have probed these questions*—at least not very much: Who am I? What am I to do? What is God calling me to do? How and where do I find the answers? You might not realize the relationship between these questions.

3. You may be just trying to *survive* day by day. You have bills to pay, kids to feed, and a job. The rest of your hours are spent managing and maintaining. Literally, for some, you may be living in poverty or dangerous circumstances.

4. *Practicality* may be driving you. You may be aimed at obtaining a degree and landing a "good" job. Your goal in life may be to meet the right person and get married. Perhaps the idea of owning your own home and paying the mortgage is driving you. Maybe getting your kids involved with the right activities and paying for them is your objective. Perhaps you are shooting for twenty years with the company. Pursuing something unrelated to your degree may seem like a waste. Living in an alternate way is difficult to imagine. Some risks might be required, and risks just plain are not *practical*. There was time when practicality was driving me.

5. If you were to modify your life, you may feel that you have *failed* in some way or that you have missed the point in the past.

6. You may be controlled by *others' expectations* of you. If you were to live a bit differently from what others might expect, you may be afraid that others will think poorly or even belittle you.

7. Maybe *fear* of some kind has taken the lead in your life and is paralyzing you.

8. You may be caught up in *attaining "success"* as defined by the rest of the world.

9. You may be overly concerned about the *missing piece on your résumé*. You may think, If I just do this one thing, then my résumé will be complete.

10. You may feel *just plain stuck* with no other available options. Sometimes, I have felt this way.

11. You may excel at many things. However, you never have *invested the time to ask*: What do I enjoy? What brings me

inner joy? What would bring meaning and purpose and cause me to be fulfilled?

12. You may think, *Enjoy what I am doing? Is this possible?* You may think that it is only an unattainable luxury to have meaning and inner joy.

Do you see yourself in any of these hindrances? Knowing God's call and answering those two key questions are critical for you. Therefore, I urge you to find ways to neutralize and minimize these mental hurdles. You may need to recognize the toll you are paying. Maybe you need to make a personal commitment. Perhaps others need to encourage you.

God's Call

**Know   Follow   Uniquely Serve
Jesus Christ**

WHO AM I??

Dreams
Passions

SPIRITUAL
GIFTS

Experience

Interests

Knowledge

Personality

Talents
Skills
Abilities

Creativity

Identity

**Receiving
God's Guidance**

Burdens
for the
World

Listening to God's Word

**Listening to Trusted
Family and Friends**

What Am I To Do??

Where Is My Call Carried Out??

Family   Work

Church

World

Diagram A

Because of these hurdles, perhaps your life is not built around how God has custom designed and called you. Diagram A provides a picture for investigating these important matters. The top of the diagram outlines many characteristics of your custom design, focusing upon: *Who am I?* In turn, the bottom of the diagram sketches the various arenas of your life, addressing: *What am I to do?* The middle of the diagram tackles the searching process: *How and where do I find the answers?* As you explore the various vantage points of this diagram, you will receive greater clarity and vision. Somewhere in the midst of this milieu, I have the hopeful expectation that you will hear God's call.

God calls. God has called. God is calling. God will call. God calls.
These words are very comforting and freeing for me! Though call can be a noun, it is most fundamentally a verb. The subject of the verb "call" is always God—a living, active, and personal God. This knowledge will allow you to rest and wait for God to reveal to you the way. After all, you have a big God. Your God has created the universe, all time and space, and knows each little detail of it all, including each little detail about your custom design (Psalm 139). Even when you are not paying any attention to God and are totally wrapped up in the concerns and worries of life, God is still at work. Despite these distractions, God still calls to you. Miraculously, God desires to empower you and work through you to realize his perfect plan for all creation—giving you all that you require.

"Now to him who is able to do immeasurably more than all we ask or imagine, according to his power that is at work within us, to him be glory in the church and in Christ Jesus throughout all generations, for ever and ever" (Ephesians 3:20, NIV).

Custom Designed and Called to be a Unique Child of God

You are called to be a unique child of God. All by itself, carefully examining your custom design can be fulfilling and fun.

Analyzing a portrait of a face such as the *Mona Lisa* is a study in character and personality. Artists have always known this fact. Countless essays have been written on the shape of Mona Lisa's smile.

All faces have two eyes, a nose, a mouth, two ears, skin, and a bone structure. Though these features are limited, no two faces are exactly the same. How these attributes are shaped and stand in relation to each other create a very unique facial profile. In fact, a face most readily identifies anyone.

Not unlike your facial features, the characteristics along

the top of Diagram A form and shape a one-of-a-kind "pro-file" of you. Similar in nature to a résumé, each will highlight distinctive strengths and qualities of your custom design. As you prayerfully study your unique individuality, you will no doubt uncover some significant discoveries. Jot them in the spaces. This will be valuable work. So, let's get started!

Talents, Skills and Abilities

Talents are aptitudes given by God at your birth, causing you to excel at certain activities with an unusual and unexplainable superior quality. You may be musically talented. You may have the gift of gab and can easily carry on a conversation. You may be a complex thinker. You may be a gifted dancer. You may be unusually good at comedy. You may have profound intelligence. Talents are not just artistic in nature. When you engage in your talents, you feel joy, and they put a smile on your face. Think about times in your life when something you have done has energized you.

On the other hand, skills and abilities are learned in a classroom or through experience. They are acquired by observation or because of a mentor. Skills and abilities enhance and complement your God-given talents. You may be an attentive listener. Through piano lessons and practice, you gained techniques, developing your musical talent. A coach enhanced your athletic ability. You may have learned plumbing skills through a combination of trial and error, and the clerk at the hardware store.

Maybe you think that you have no talents, but they are there. Review the list of skills, talents, and abilities found in

Appendix A. Then, show it to others who know you. Others will recognize your talents and skills, calling attention to them. Ask others what they observe in you. You will always have talents yet to be discovered. Throughout your life, you will acquire still more skills and abilities.

I can plan, teach, and train with an ear open to God's leading. I can creatively organize details. I am an inventor. I can troubleshoot. I enjoy preparing presentations. I can write. I enjoy dramatic reading. I can creatively administrate by custom designing a team. I enjoy design. I learned to be frugal from my parents. In college, I learned accounting and other business skills. I have read about investing. As a result, I am a skillful budgeter and financial planner. A more complete list of talents, skills, and abilities can be found in the book, *What Color Is Your Parachute?* by Richard Nelson Bolles.

Knowledge

What is stored in your head? Knowledge is cognitive information, understanding, expertise, or wisdom. Knowledge is gathered from a host of sources: classrooms, life experience, significant mentors, workshops, seminars, hands-on learning, reading, or research. This knowledge may be practical knowledge, common sense knowledge, or knowledge related to a field of study. There is also spiritual knowledge, biblical knowledge, and knowledge or insight related to life—for example, family, relationships, or health. Think about your classroom experiences. What have you learned from your parents, friends, and others? What books have been significant for you and why? What have you gained from work and volunteer experiences?

Through my chaplaincy experience, I learned a lot about conflict resolution and relationship dynamics. Every day I grow in my knowledge of the Scriptures. When I was an engineer, my boss and others taught me much about visionary thinking. I continue to learn about visionary thinking. I know how to creatively manage a project.

Past Experiences—Positive and Negative

You have a history. A multitude of experiences have defined and shaped your unique individuality. Relive your biography a bit. What has been meaningful? What has not been meaningful? What has been painful? Taking inventory of both your positive and negative experiences can be helpful.

Recalling your negative experiences will reveal important insights related to your identity—who you are and who you are not. Further, if a negative occurrence was painful, you may have valuable wisdom as a result of persevering through this incident. For example, you may understand much about grief because a close family member died. God may use your experience and insight to bring healing to another. Thus, God can transform a difficult experience into something positive—an asset. Further, through reminding you of a harmful occurrence, God can bring a greater measure of healing to you. As a result, God will increase your confidence and hope as you walk into the future—more on this later. Generally, you have personal experience in four different arenas of life.

1. *Work:* List all of your jobs since you were very young. Review all the various activities and tasks connected with

these jobs. Attempt to rate all of these activities, tasks, and experiences from one to five according to their level of fulfillment and enjoyment. My fifteen plus employment stints all highlight various characteristics of my custom design.

2. *Family, Friends, and Home:* Consider important relationships in your life. What are the positives? What are the negatives? What are the tasks and activities that are involved in maintaining a home? What do you enjoy? What do you not enjoy? If you are married, perhaps you might discuss these questions with your spouse. Who are important life mentors for you? Why? What would you like to improve or change in your home or relationships? What would it take to create more meaningful relationships?

3. *Neighborhood, Community, and World:* What has been your involvement with your neighborhood, community, and world? What have you learned? What volunteer work have you done? What has been fulfilling? Why? What was not fulfilling? Why?

4. *God Experience and Church:* Tap into your spiritual journey. Recall your God story. Consider your God encounters and your God sightings. Name your mountaintop experiences. How has God worked in your life? How have you served God through the years? Rate these service experiences from one to five according to their level of fulfillment and enjoyment.

Observe common themes in your history. Common connections will give insight into your custom design. They will point the way to your future.

Interests and Hobbies

God is even interested in your leisure activities. I enjoy sewing, making gifts, creatively planning a celebration, and several sports—football, baseball, hockey, and basketball. One of my friends loves baseball. Similar to me, he also enjoys teaching about God's call. While coaching baseball, he uses this moment of opportunity to teach kids about God's call. God may have a meaningful purpose for your interests and hobbies.

Creativity

God is infinitely original. Think about the leaves throughout time. No two are the same. You were created in the image of God (Genesis 1:27), and therefore, you are a creative being. Creativity is about the new, different, and "out of the box." Think about how you employ your creativity. You may be a creative gift giver, a creative homemaker, a creative parent, or creative in some other respect. Because you are not an artist, musician, poet, or actor, you may not think that you are creative. You may need to rediscover your creative edge. Your Creator will inspire originality and creativity in you. I am a creative thinker, troubleshooter, and problem solver.

Personality

Pick your personality preferences out of the following orientations. Even though you may be able to function quite well within either orientation, usually you will have a preference one way or the other. I have asterisked my own preferences.

*Task-oriented vs. People-oriented
*Structure vs. Flexible
*Planner vs. Spontaneity
Big Picture vs. Details*
*Intuitive vs. Sensory
*Hard Worker vs. Rest and Play
*Energized by Solitude vs. Energized by Socializing
*Be in charge vs. Have someone tell you what to do

In addition, you may prefer working with certain age groups—children or teens or adults or retirees or families, or you might not have a preference for a certain age group. I prefer working with older teens and adults of any age. You also may prefer working alone or in pairs or with a small group or a large group, or you might not have a preference. Though I am very capable of working with a larger group, I prefer working with a smaller group of people or even alone.

You may believe that your preferences are ideal, or conversely, that somehow you are not the ultimate orientation. All of these preferences have both their advantages and disadvantages. My husband and I are polar opposites on a couple of these preferences. He is Mr. Flexibility, and I am Ms. Structure. When our family is on vacation, flexibility can be a wonderful gift. When something needs to get accomplished in a timely manner, structure is indispensable. Having people with various preferences is actually helpful, creating a beneficial and effective balance. Knowing your preferences will allow you to work more effectively with others, both compensating for your weaknesses and valuing rather than critiquing others' differences. You may even avoid conflict by recognizing your own and others' preferences. To learn more about your personality, consider taking a Myers-Briggs personality profile.

Identity

To join a fraternity or a sorority, first someone is initiated. When initiated, they become a member, taking on the identity of that group. At my college, you became a Theta or Phi Beta Kappa. In a similar manner, baptism has been labeled initiation. When you were baptized, you were initiated, and God gave you an incredible identity. You became a *child* of God, a saint, a steward, an anointed one, a disciple and much more. Presently some of these powerful designations may mean little to you, but we will investigate and find out more about your incredible identity. Like the prodigal son, you may have wandered so far away from your heavenly Father and his home that it is almost as if you are no longer a son—a *child* of the Father; however, you are still a son and you can return and live again in the fullness of your identity (Luke 15:11). If you are not baptized, you might want to find out more from a pastor or priest.

Resources

What has God given to you? What possessions do you own—like clothing, luxury items, tools, and other belongings? How about your home and everything in it? Property? Monetary resources? Investments? Inventory your "goods." How could all of these be utilitarian tools to promote purposeful living? I am blessed with a beautiful home. God has increased my investments. My unique attributes are assets. Wise living is a goal of mine. Whether you have a lot or a little, God needs people of all economic standings. What would you feel comfortable sharing and with whom? Everyone? How could God more meaningfully make use of your home? What are your desires as far as giving? Investing in important initiatives can be very fulfilling. This may be why God has blessed you with many of your resources. What is squandered in wasteful wanton living?

If you have been given more than enough, you may fear that God will take it away by asking you to live akin to a pauper. Remember, God does not initiate this kind of fear. For now keep a simple list of your possessions and resources, assuming that none of these fears will come true. Powerful and practical insights to produce a wise economy of life will be offered in a later chapter.

Dreams and Passions

If you were caught daydreaming, what movie would be playing in your mind? Envision yourself doing something incredibly fulfilling—something where you lose all sense of time or where you are driven and significantly motivated. What creates enthusiasm, energy, and excitement for you? Paint a picture of your passions. What would this look like? Pay attention to passions from your past. I envision people living out God's call, positively impacting the world. I dream of a church that is custom designed around unique people created and called by God. Allow yourself to dream. Dreams can become reality. Sometimes God may tweak or alter them a bit. When have you caught a glimpse of your dreams?

Burdens for the World

God pours his love into your heart and causes it to ache with his compassion. You may have a deep concern for the hungry or the poor or the lost. You may have unexplainable compassion for the handicapped or those in prison or people with AIDS. People who do not know significance in life may disturb you. Ineffective churches or governments may bother you. Certain moral issues or the seeming absence of truth may burden you. The list of problems could go on and on. When you lie awake at night, what concerns or bothers you the most? Which of these concerns is within your sphere of influence? If you could only make one or two or three major changes in the lives of people in this world, what would you choose? To some degree, I am burdened by all the problems of the world. Further, I am burdened by the American church's ineffectiveness in solving these problems and transforming the world. Therefore, I believe people knowing God's call is crucial to making a difference. We will think about passions and burdens in the great reversal chapter.

Spiritual Gifts

Amazingly, spiritual gifts already are functioning in your life. These gifts are specific endowments given by God's Spirit that quite naturally (really supernaturally) motivate, empower, and create competence—equipping you to serve God and others in everyday life. Like the bones in your face, spiritual gifts are the supporting structure for your unique profile. Because spiritual gifts are so critical for understanding your custom design and call, the whole next chapter will be devoted to these exciting gifts. My spiritual gifts are teaching, leadership, and administration. God frequently manifests in me the spiritual gifts of wisdom, discernment, and faith. Unknowingly, these same spiritual gifts may be functioning in your life.

Who are you? God the Father has called you to be his unique child. Indeed, you are a masterpiece, intricately created with a multitude of magnificent features. The good news is that your "custom design" is intimately related to what God is calling you to *do*.

"For it was you who formed my inward parts; you knit me together in my mother's womb. I praise you, for I am fearfully and wonderfully made. Wonderful are your works; that I know very well. My frame was not hidden from you when I was being made in secret, intricately woven in the depths of the earth" (Psalm 139:13–15, NRSV).

Called to be Gifted and Empowered

Caution! Perhaps these words of warning are pertinent to you:

"Do not neglect your gift ... which was given to you" (1 Timothy 4:14, NRSV).

"Now concerning spiritual gifts, brothers and sisters, I do not want you to be uninformed" (1 Corinthians 12:1, NRSV).

Even though throughout the centuries God has given spiritual gifts, these words alert us to some dangers. Bill Hybels, pastor of one of the largest church gatherings in the USA, relays his own experience of growing up in great churches with great pastors and never hearing about spiritual gifts.[1] Though this danger may be less common today than in years past, still all too many neglect or remain uninformed about their spiritual gifts. Remember your spiritual gifts are a crucial part of your custom design. Understanding them is consequential.

Yet another danger is to assume that spiritual gifts are only pertinent while at church. However, perhaps unknowingly, your spiritual gifts function in your family, work, neighborhood, community, world, and all that you do day by day. In all of these settings, your spiritual gifts will intensely motivate, energize, and even drive you to accomplish certain things, and conversely, not to do other things. Yes! Some of these gifts are already operating in you. Discovering and identifying your gifts will create more focus, fulfillment, and effectiveness in all the "doings" of your life. In a bit, I will introduce you to my friends—real people who so aptly illustrate how spiritual gifts function in all of life.

Still yet another danger is to possess only a cursory knowledge of these gifts. While understanding next to nothing about spiritual gifts, I experienced speaking in tongues. To me, this gift seemed very unusual, bizarre, and even extreme. Something of this sort was not what I remotely desired. For a long time, I had no desire to find out about spiritual gifts. This fear is actually quite common. Like me, fear and misinformation may be preventing you from discovering something very inspiring, exciting, and important about yourself.

Still after many years, I never cease to be amazed by people's energy level when they first find out about spiritual gifts. Many begin a meaningful and even fun quest to better comprehend how these gifts function. Quite miraculously, some— like my friends David, Steve, and Dick—go from having little to no understanding of their gifts to later doing undreamed of endeavors. Now David, Dick, and Steve are all enthusiastic spiritual gift advocates and teachers. God calls and empowers ordinary people like you, equipping you with spiritual gifts.

Definitions

There are three correct, but different definitions of the term spiritual gifts. You will understand more about your own spiritual gifts by knowing the distinctions between these definitions.

1. Everything good in your life is a gift from God and therefore is a spiritual gift. This is very true!

2. When you allow God's Spirit to fill you, then your actions, talents, skills and really everything can be empowered by the Spirit and thus operate like a spiritual gift. This is also very true!

3. *Spiritual gifts are specific competencies endowed by God's Spirit that naturally (supernaturally) motivate and empower you to serve God and others in everyday life.* We will focus on the gifts founds in these scriptures: 1 Corinthians 12:7–11 and 12:28–31, Ephesians 4:11–13, and Romans 12:4–8.

Though other spiritual gifts teachers may have differences of approach, most would agree that these gifts are competencies endowed by God's Spirit to empower and equip us to serve.

When are spiritual gifts given? The Scriptures imply that they are given at baptism (1 Corinthians 12:13). Some say that they are given when people are created. If granted at birth, then perhaps they are empowered for spiritual purposes when a believer is baptized with water and the Spirit.

Overview of the Biblical Spiritual Gifts

So, which gifts belong to you? As each gift is simply defined, contemplate these questions: Do I have the qualities and behaviors that mark this gift? Do my skills, abilities, and talents match-up? To which gifts am I drawn? What do others see in me?

Pay close attention to the differences between these four distinctive types: functional gifts, functional and equipping gifts, manifestation gifts, and gifts of expression.

Functional Gifts

Like human body parts functioning all together, we are called to be the "body of Christ"—the physical presence of Jesus on earth right now (1 Corinthians 12). We each are spiritually endowed to be a unique part of his body. Knowing your combination of gifts will define and shape your part and function. These gifts will intensely motivate you, drawing you to certain activities while being uninterested in others. Two to four of these functional gifts already belong to you.

Service (Romans 12:7): Behind the scenes, Leroy is extraordinarily skilled at construction. You might spot him fixing many and various things that are begging for attention. People with the service gift show their love for God and others by doing "nuts and bolts" tasks. "Nuts and bolts" tasks are behind-the-scenes small, but very necessary and defined tasks that in many instances hold together (like nuts and bolts) a group, event, or project. For example, people with this gift may enjoy setting up or taking down for an event, running errands, cleaning, yard work, fixing and maintaining a facility or equipment, or preparing and serving food.

Donna serves and works as a schoolteacher. In her spare time, she is often found doing dishes or setting tables for large events. She may be found preparing and helping children with craft projects while learning about God's word.

Encouragement (Romans 12:8): Cathy almost always has a smile on her face. As a hospital surgical nurse, she serves God by lifting the spirits of others. She is joyful and genuinely positive as she encourages the musically talented to employ their gifts. She is positive even when she is being negative.

People with the encouragement gift are motivated to build up other people, giving them inner courage. Functioning as cheerleaders, they often have the right word for a given situation. They are very genuinely positive. They notice when others are discouraged. Joel gives inner courage through his prayers and wise counsel.

Mercy (Romans 12:8): Cindy is a trained and certified sign language interpreter, serving the deaf patients at an inner city hospital. Now she contemplates becoming a chaplain for those same patients. She also exercises great care and compassion for poor people.

People with the mercy gift have a deep concern and compassion, particularly for people who may be on the fringes or ostracized or disadvantaged in some way or in need of compassion. For example, concern could be directed toward one or more of the following: the handicapped, the elderly, the poor, the oppressed, the homeless, those with addictions, those in prison, those who have screwed up their lives, or those with AIDS—to name a few examples. Frequently people with a mercy gift will be easily moved to tears.

Candy is a speech therapist at a Veteran's Administration

hospital. Compassionately and patiently, she works with those whose speech has become severely handicapped by debilitating injury. Candy also has a great heart for immigrants and elderly people, demonstrating this in many sacrificial, hands-on and practical ways.

Administration or Administrative Leadership (1 Corinthians 12:28): Dick is a school principal, managing the staff and educational activities of many children. He coordinates large events for his church and other organizations as well. Faithfully, he brings together all the needed people and tasks, creating an enjoyable experience for all.

People with the administration gift are able to coordinate and manage all the necessary tasks, details, people, and resources in order to make something happen. Organized and detail-oriented are terms describing this gift. People with this gift may have either a people-oriented focus or a behind-the-scenes task-oriented focus. Some may have both orientations. The biblical Greek word for this gift literally means governing leadership. Even though the biblical Greek word most often is translated as "administration," this gift is also a leadership gift—though different in nature from the "leadership" gift.

Kathy is a certified public accountant who works as an auditor for an accounting firm. Sharing the love of God, she constantly encourages and prays for her fellow employees and others who might be struggling. As an accountant for her firm, church, and another non-profit service organization, she is swift and accurate in holding together all the financial details, records, and reports, effectively communicating with all the necessary parties.

Leadership or Big Picture Leadership (Romans 12:8): David

directs a very large worldwide child sponsorship agency. For years, he has promoted the vision of children living without poverty. People with the big picture leadership gift have a God-given authority and ability to influence people. "God-given" implies that these people are able to influence quite naturally without control and high-energy emotion though they might have these tendencies. They are usually thinking or operating ahead of everyone else. They are big picture thinkers. The biblical Greek word for this gift literally means to stand in front of others.

Mary has served in the political arena for many years, first as an aide to a United States Senator and then as a vice president of public policy for a very large urban health care system. She advocates for more effective health care, networking with prominent physicians and health care professionals. In her spare time with some of these same people, she leads mission endeavors, partnering with hospitals and clinics in impoverished places all over the world.

Giving (Romans 12:8): Steve feels blessed to be a founding partner and leader of a very large corporate law firm, specializing in complex business conflicts. God has endowed him with much. He generously gives his resources to invest in God's work not only through his church, but also a non-profit organization helping people find meaning and significance in life.

People with the giving gift have a God-given deep resolve to meet the financial and material needs of God's work, enabling it to continue. God inspires a desire to give over and above the average committed Christian. As a result, people endowed in this way often give over the tithe (ten percent). The giving gift operates through one or more of the following means: acquisition of wealth, voluntary and sacrificial austerity, maximization of resources, giving up financial gain, benevolent hospitality, and even celibacy. No two people with the giving gift will express the gift in the same way or support identical needs. Some with the gift may have wealth while others have very modest means.

Out of personal desire, Cheryl gave up her well-paying position as the director of data processing at a hospital in order to become an administrator of her church, earning about half the pay. She loves her new position. When she receives a bonus, she often buys new equipment for her church office even though she lives very modestly. Linda is single and views her singleness as a gift, allowing her to spend many hours praying for others. At the same time, Linda works and serves as an oncology nurse. By living simply and investing wisely, she gives about thirty percent of her income to the Lord's work!

Hospitality (1 Peter 4:9–10, Romans 12:13): Fred was an easy-going kind of a guy with a twinkle in his eye. As the payroll department manager for a very populous urban county, all of his co-workers especially enjoyed working with him. Then he moved to a new city. A short time later, he knew everyone in his neighborhood–sometimes a rare incidence in modern America. When he died, his family received many cards and letters saying how Fred always made them feel "comfortable."

People with the hospitality gift are intensely motivated to love outsiders, making them feel safe, connected, comfortable, and at ease. They are very welcoming. The biblical Greek word for hospitality literally means "love of the stranger." This gift can be expressed either through conversation and caring for people or by creating a comfortable and welcoming atmosphere.

Go to almost any restaurant with Janice and she has already befriended most of the employees and seems to know many other people there as well. She promotes friendship by throwing big parties at her house, often inviting new people. Janice is a school librarian, and of course the children think she is the best. On behalf of her church, she encourages faith by leading a women's book study at a local restaurant. At all of these places, she is constantly and continually inviting new people to her church gathering with a great degree of success.

When we first moved to town, Carolee and Dwayne offered the upstairs of their house to my family of six for no less than three months. They did not know our family, but we soon knew each other. We ate and lived together while being encouraged by their generosity. In spite of our trying, they would accept very little compensation in return for their time and inconvenience. After those three months, I sure felt less like a "stranger."

Missionary (Acts 1:8, Matthew 28:18–20): When Marian and Keith retired they went to Bolivia on a mission endeavor, serving as the official photographers. Following this experience until she died at ninety-five years young, Marian used "hats" to raise thousands of dollars for world mission at a very small church in a very small town, far surpassing much larger churches in more populated places. Every year, the "hat lady" would pray about her approach. Sometimes she would wake up in the middle of the night with an idea, and then with her very playful and fun personality, she would execute. You are never too old to use your gifts!

People with the missionary gift have a deep appreciation for other cultures. Sometimes they have a God-given sense of adventure and openness to going anywhere. They also may easily learn foreign languages.

Suzanne regularly travels to Haiti to encourage her partner church there. Using her physical therapy skills, she once spent six weeks serving children with debilitating handicaps in China, doing all of this on her own nickel. With others, she settled in a Haitian refugee family in the United States.

Intercession (Luke 2:36–38): Bill constantly prays while he paints, changes light bulbs, and serves food. People with the intercession gift are intensely motivated to pray. For extended periods of times, they pray for people, places, and circumstances. When their mental energy is not required for more immediate matters, God naturally will turn their attention to praying about anything and everything as led by his Spirit.

Zelda very often prays for her country while pulling weeds in the parking lot or straightening rows of chairs. Weekly, she sends notes of encouragement to many, praying for them as she writes. With others, Bill and Zelda are behind the scenes, constantly praying for others—maybe even for you!

Functional and Equipping Gifts

These next functional gifts prepare people to do God's work (Ephesians 4:11–12).

Shepherd (Ephesians 4:11): Toni recently became a massage therapist. She enjoys bringing healing to her clients through her massage while silently praying for them. She has a joyful, inviting spirit as she encourages and cares for others in many and various ways. Throughout the years, she has sought out many wandering spirits by patiently loving and prodding them in the right direction. Using her musical gifts, she encourages people and builds relationships by leading choirs and other ensembles. She is a tremendous mother to her own kids as well as many others.

People with the shepherd gift are concerned about the spiritual nurture of people offered through relationship building. In Ezekiel 34, while critiquing the shepherds of Israel, God characterizes a true shepherd. Shepherds are those who seek the lost, strengthen the weak, heal the sick, bind up the injured, and bring back the strayed. Even though the biblical Greek word literally means shepherd, often it is translated as pastor. This translation can create confusion. Having this gift does not mean that someone should be the pastor of a church. In any church gathering, several people who are not "pastors" will have this gift. In addition, many "pastors" do not have this gift.

David is a purchasing agent who will often give his time to visit someone in the hospital or make a phone call to someone who is hurting or on the fringes. He is constantly checking up on the staff of his church, supporting and encouraging them.

Serving as a public school teacher, children's choir director, and mom to many, Kelly easily endears children with her kindness and genuine care.

Teacher (Ephesians 4:11, Romans 12:7, 1 Corinthians 12:28): For many years, Steve has mentored new attorneys at his law firm, encouraging them to excellence. He has coached kids, including his own son, in the art of baseball. Now he is especially motivated to teach people about God's call, and in turn, how to wisely use their time and resources to live a life worthy of God's call.

People with the teaching gift are concerned about bringing spiritual understanding with the result that God's insight and wisdom are revealed and people are transformed. Often they are concerned about spiritual depth. They deeply desire to help people learn about the kingdom of God. People with this gift are very motivated to learn themselves and motivated to impart spiritual knowledge that results in personal revelation and insight.

Carolee serves as a school librarian in an ethnically diverse school, increasing literacy with children by encouraging them to improve their reading skills. For many years, she has combined her creativity, humor, and love of fun by joyfully teaching a group of elderly women in another of her loves—God's word.

Evangelist (Ephesians 4:11): Bitania grew up in Ethiopia where her family experienced oppression and persecution. With practically nothing in hand, her family left and came to New York City. It was a hard journey. Now, she feels privileged to share her infectious zeal for Jesus whether out and about, or at home with her four children. Jesus has transformed her life, and she has a hard time containing the hope that she has received. She offers it through words and actions to others including her clients at the old folks' care facility where she works.

People with the evangelist gift have a God-given ability to bring about the fruits of conversion, repentance, and trust in the gospel of Jesus way beyond the average committed Christian. Like Billy Graham, some evangelists preach to large groups with unexplainable miraculous results. When a church gathering grows quickly, usually the primary preacher has this gift. Still others use their gift in one-on-one interactions, and they may never speak in front of a crowd. Some use both avenues.

Prophecy (Ephesians 4:11, Romans 12:6, 1 Corinthians 12:28): Wilhart had a deep seated concern for moral purity in the world. He was dogged in his pursuit even into his later years of life. Some thought that he was a nuisance. Occasionally, he was.

People with the prophetic gift have a deep concern for biblical truth, authority, and, as a result, ethics, and morality. They are not afraid to speak up when biblical truth is at stake. Oftentimes they might even speak on behalf of God. Sometimes they may be critical or abrasive. Martin Luther posted ninety-five theses for debate and found himself endlessly defending fundamental and scriptural principles related to the Gospel. Martin Luther King shared an uncontainable concern for the equal rights of all people. Both suffered great persecution as a result. One had threats against his life, and the other lost his life. Were they right about everything? No, but they were right about some vital issues.

Daniel, a person of generosity, is totally put off by people trusting in themselves and their possessions—in other words, idolatry.

Apostle (Ephesians 4:11, 1 Corinthians 12:28): An apostle is a leader of leaders. They are highly respected by leaders of many faith backgrounds or traditions, often having a worldwide influence. People with a role of this nature such as the pope or a bishop will not necessarily have this gift. The apostle Paul identified these marks of an apostle: signs, wonders, and miracles (2 Corinthians 12:12). This title is reserved for a small few.

Manifestation Gifts

Manifestation gifts complement and support your functional gifts. Certain manifestation gifts correlate and frequently occur with certain functional gifts. For example, people with a functional gift of leadership or administration will have frequent manifestations of wisdom, discernment, or the spiritual gift of faith. Those with a shepherd gift may have frequent manifestations of the gifts of knowledge or healing. People with the intercession gift may have frequent manifestations of speaking in tongues.

"Manifestation" is a label derived from the words preceding the spiritual gifts listed in 1 Corinthians 12:7–11: "To each is given the manifestation of the Spirit for the common good" (1 Corinthians 12:7). The biblical Greek word for manifestation means to make visible or reveal. Thus these gifts reveal or make visible the Holy Spirit's power and work in a situation. In other words, when these gifts operate, God's supernatural activity is obvious. All of these gifts have an unexplainable aspect to them.

Wisdom (1 Corinthians 12:8) occurs when God inspires a person with supernatural insight and understanding in order to determine what to do or say in a particular situation or in general. Quite amazingly, an engineer and handyman named Rudy ingeniously solved many complicated issues in his church gathering. Steve has what he calls "glimpses" where he suddenly knows how to approach complex issues in his leadership role. He knows that God is the source of these glimpses.

Knowledge (1 Corinthians 12:8) occurs when God inspires a person to see, know, or proclaim the truth without knowing it in any way except by supernatural revelation. God also may inspire a person with this gift to master and apply the truths of God's word in an amazingly helpful way. Without anyone telling her, newly married Ardis knew that her husband had died. She even began to cry, grieving as God prepared her for this shocking news. Miles away, an accident at the lake cabin claimed his life.

Faith (1 Corinthians 12:9) occurs when God gives a person eyes to see and know the Holy Spirit's intentions and unexplainable faith to believe these intentions will happen without any kind of tangible evidence to support their transpiring. David had steadfast inner confidence that he would be offered an ideal job with the park service. He continued to pray, trusting that it would come to pass, and it did. Steve was certain that God would provide a large sum of money, eliminating a long-standing debt of his church. Sure enough, it happened. Here the word "faith" is used differently from how we typically use the term, e.g., saving faith.

Visionaries are people who have frequent manifestations of the "faith" gift. In other words, God gives these people a vision that involves not just oneself—one's own gifts, resources, and time—but other people as well and the "faith" to believe this vision will come to pass.

Victor is a visionary. Part of his personal vision is to facilitate and increase the speed of Bible translation. He uses his gifts to enable a larger vision, making the scriptures available in all languages. He designs alphabets and fonts for non-Roman languages and develops the technology for them to be used on a computer. He now trains and leads a team of people dedicated to this endeavor with a very large Bible translation organization. He has greatly influenced literacy, and even pioneered and made available innovative computer technology. As a result, he is invited to speak at technology gatherings all over the world. He and his family live simply, enabling his work to happen.

Healing (1 Corinthians 12:9) occurs when God, through the prayer and actions of a person, brings supernatural healing and restoration of wholeness to another. "Supernatural" implies that God heals outside of the God-created natural body processes and medicine. Through this gift, God may also magnify the God-created natural process of healing and medicine that is also amazing. Using his shepherd gift, Joel frequently visits people with health concerns and prays for their healing. Sometimes unexplainably with tingling in his fingertips, healing happens instantaneously. In these less frequent instances, the words of his prayer and the desires of his heart do not differ from other times when he prays for healing.

Discernment (1 Corinthians 12:10) occurs when God allows a person to supernaturally sense in an accurate manner whether a situation has its source in Satan, human flesh, the world, or God. Hanna sometimes senses deceitful motives. Sometimes she even receives helpful wisdom to combat these motives. Later, she finds out that she was correct.

Miracles (1 Corinthians 12:10) occur when God through a person introduces supernatural intervention into the natural God-created course of cause and effect. Jesus' miracles always brought glory to God, and blessing to people. A priest once served ham to an impoverished and hungry multitude in a dirty border town. The priest kept slicing and slicing and slicing and slicing the ham, and it never ran out.

Prophecy (1 Corinthians 12:10) occurs when a person is used as a mouthpiece to receive and then directly reveal or speak a message from God. Like Old Testament prophecies, often it is in the "first person" because God is speaking with words like, "Thus says the Lord: I am…" The test of a prophet is whether his words come true and bring about their intent; therefore, I reserve judgment by not giving modern-day examples.

Tongues (1 Corinthians 12:10) occurs when God supernaturally and unexplainably allows a person to speak in an earthly or heavenly language for the purpose of prayer—to talk to God, hear from our Lord, or offer praise to God. Speaking in tongues may be inaudible or audible. It is controllable by the persons speaking. If it is audible to others, the spiritual gift of interpretation is almost always required.

When Julie was a child, she would go to her favorite spot and pray. Sometimes, she would pray not with English, but with varying sounds. When she was an adult, she was convinced that she prayed in tongues. She still prays in tongues. Her gift of tongues complements her intercession gift.

Interpretation of tongues (1 Corinthians 12:10) occurs when God gives a person the exact meaning or translation of the words spoken using the spiritual gift of tongues. Whenever Anne sees a car accident, she is often led to pray in tongues. When Anne prays in tongues, she simultaneously prays in English with her mind. She is convinced that God is using her thoughts to interpret her prayer in tongues.

Remember these supernatural manifestation gifts support, complement, and may even correlate with your functional gifts.

Gifts of Expression

Gifts of expression are God-given talents empowered and used by the Holy Spirit to do God's work. Filled with the Holy Spirit, Bezalel and Oholiab created beautiful art for the tabernacle:

> *Then Moses said to the Israelites: See the Lord has called by name Bezalel ... he has filled him with divine spirit, with skill, intelligence, and knowledge in every kind of craft, to devise artistic designs ... And he has inspired him to teach, both him and Oholiab ... He has filled them with skill to do every kind of work done by an artisan or by a designer or by an embroiderer or by a weaver—by any sort of artisan or skilled designer.*
>
> Exodus 35:30–35 (NRSV)

When you allow the Spirit of God to fill your life, then your actions, talents, skills, and really everything can be empowered by the Spirit of God. There are literally millions of spiritual gifts of expression.

Music (Asaph—1 Chronicles 25:1): Johann Sebastian Bach certainly was inspired by God to compose and make magnificent music, moving many throughout the years to experience God's Word, beauty, and presence.

Arts and crafts (Bezalel and Oholiab—Exodus 35:30–35): Judy cooks tasty and attractive food for large gatherings.

She once baked pies with young children to raise funds for renovating a nursery. Like Bezalel and Oholiab, she creates beautiful tapestries for God's sanctuary. Judy will prepare food and crafts for the "Make-a-Valentine" luncheon to raise funds for her church's mission efforts.

Writing (Isaiah—Isaiah 1:1, 6:1–13): In the middle of the night, Susan once woke up and was inspired to write a children's play. She felt God's incredible presence as she wrote.

Speech (Isaiah—Isaiah 61): Carolee has a wonderful gift of storytelling that she uses to bring joy to others.

Drama (Song of Solomon): Many times, God's Spirit inspired Claudia to both create and produce extraordinary and meaningful dramatic productions and puppet plays.

Dance (David—2 Samuel 5:3, 6:14): Lauren is a young adult. She dances with such wonderful beauty and grace. Dance, prayer, and worship blend together for Lauren. She longs to be a Broadway dancer, hoping to shine light where there is darkness with both her dance and fellow performers.

Craftsmanship or manual crafts (Huram-abi—2 Chronicles 2:13–14): Wade is a "dirt man" who skillfully uses his contouring and landscaping skills while encouraging his clients with God's joy and love.

Hopefully you felt inspired by all of my friends. There are a multitude of uses for every gift. So, try opportunities to which you are attracted or drawn. Notice your level of energy, fulfillment, and effectiveness. As you undertake opportunities, others will notice your gifts. Listen to what they affirm in you.

Identifying Your Spiritual Gifts

Use is a key word. Through using your spiritual gifts, you not only will clarify them, but you will understand how they function in your life, and more importantly, how God is calling you to employ them in the future. Besides trying opportunities, the acronym shown in Diagram B outlines other helpful ways to identify your spiritual gifts.

Completing a spiritual gifts inventory is a common way to begin discerning your gifts. An inventory is only an indicator. Though its results may not exactly pinpoint your spiritual gifts, it will launch a very motivational discovery process. Beginning with small steps, this process may last up to a few years. Be patient! It will be exciting and well worth it.

God is

R — **Reflect and Recall** - Consider the other unique attributes of your profile and how each complements your spiritual gifts and shapes your call.

E — **Experiment and Examine** - Choose experiences that use your spiritual gifts. If you are using your spiritual gifts, you will feel excited, energized and fulfilled.

V — **Visualize and Imagine** - To which gifts are you drawn, attracted or do you feel an inner pull? As you visualize yourself using your gifts, can you imagine yourself functioning in this way?

E — **Evaluate and Reconsider** - If thinking about spiritual gifts and call is new to you, attend a workshop or talk to someone one-on-one who has an understanding of spiritual gifts.

A — **Affirmation and Input** - What do other people suggest for you, see in you or affirm in you?

L — **Listen and Pray** - Ask God, "What are you calling me to do?" Ask God for wisdom and personal vision and revelation.

I — **Inventory and Assess** - Try one or more spiritual gifts inventories.

N — **Nurture and Grow** - Most important seek to know, follow and serve Jesus.

G — **Gather and Learn** - Learn as much as you can about spiritual gifts.

YOUR SPIRITUAL GIFTS TO YOU!

DIAGRAM B

Increasing Your Effectiveness

Even in this overly busy world, people still want to serve meaningfully. Clarifying your spiritual gifts will create the freedom to more sharply focus your time and energy. You will know when to say "yes" or even "no" to various opportunities. After discerning her spiritual gifts, Tammy quit leading a Bible study so that she could devote more time to her primary passion—hospice care. No to an opportunity will lead to a yes by someone else who will enjoy, thrive, and be more effective in that opportunity.

Learning about each gift, you will increase your awareness of not only your own gifts, but also your need for others' gifts to complement and supplement your own. Everyone will be more effective.

Encouragement to Invite the Holy Spirit's Empowering

It is impossible to do much of anything for God without the power of the Holy Spirit. By inviting God's Spirit to continually fill you, your spiritual gifts and really everything in your life can be stirred and ignited with God's boundless power. When God's Spirit fills and works within you, the possibilities of what God can do with you—an ordinary, everyday person—become very extraordinary.

In the Old Testament, God called his servants. Then they were anointed with oil while God simultaneously anointed each of them with the powerful Holy Spirit, filling and empowering them to accomplish their unique callings. Though God most commonly anointed priests, prophets, and kings with the Holy Spirit, God also anointed and empowered others like the tabernacle artisans, Bezalel and Oholiab. When Jesus was baptized, he also was anointed and empowered with the Holy Spirit. He received spiritual gifts in order to accomplish his own mission and calling.

Like Jesus, you also are anointed and empowered. Amazing! Most likely at your baptism, someone prayed for you to be anointed and filled with the Holy Spirit. The Holy Spirit endowed you with spiritual gifts, equipping you to answer God's call. "Christ" and "Christian" in the biblical Greek are translated "anointed one." You are called to be an anointed one.

Early Christians who already had the Holy Spirit were encouraged in Ephesians 5:18 to not get drunk with wine, for that is excessive, but to be continually filled with the Holy Spirit. Like someone who is drunk, you are encouraged to be intoxicated with the Holy Spirit. You can ask and invite the Holy Spirit to continually fill and empower you.

During the rites of certain churches—confirmation, consecration, and ordination—people are dedicated to God's service by laying hands of blessing upon them. They are anointed with oil, and prayers are lifted to God, inviting the Holy Spirit to continually fill and empower these servants of God. In like manner, you also are a servant of God. You can invite someone to anoint you, lay hands upon you, and pray for you. They can ask the Holy Spirit to continually anoint and fill you, empowering your spiritual gifts and other unique attributes. I know that I cannot get along without the Holy Spirit's power. Therefore, whenever possible I seize the opportunity for someone to pray for God's Spirit to anoint and fill me.

Be confident! God has already supernaturally custom

designed, equipped, and empowered you with some of these extraordinary gifts. You may need a bit of time to discover them. Harnessing these gifts in everyday life with an understanding of their existence and origin will be incredibly exciting and energizing to you.

Call to Work, Family, Church, Neighborhood, Community, and World

Who are you? You are called to be a custom designed child of God, endowed with spiritual gifts and a host of other unique features. *What are you to do?* God calls you to use your custom designed individuality in the roles and arenas of your life—your work, family, church, neighborhood, community, and the world. Who you are will shed light on what you are to do.

As a new mom, I was caught in the chaos of transition. While wondering how best to invest my time, I uncovered a key insight. Our time should reflect our priorities, values, desires, and goals for life; otherwise, we will experience frustration and restlessness. While pondering my own priorities and values, I did not want my life to be merely of my own making. Therefore, I invited God to reveal my heartfelt desires, knowing that God promises to give us the desires of our hearts (Psalms 37:4–5).

I began to contemplate the various roles and arenas of my life. I started with all my relationships: God, my husband, children, parents, friends, and other extended family. Of course this covered my marriage, parenting, and the management of our home. Then, I moved to my work or vocation, including financial goals—from back then to retirement. I reflected upon my involvement in the church, community, and world. I thought about desires for intellect and learning, leisure-time hobbies, and fun. I included personal growth, and my health–emotional and physical. While reflecting upon these roles and arenas, I began to jot down my heartfelt desires for all of life. God guided my thoughts. I recorded about twenty desires, describing each one. Even then, one of my desires was to write a book with significant impact.

One day, another key insight came to me. As God was revealing my heartfelt desires, my Lord also was calling me and unfolding a vision for my life. From time to time, I still review my original list of desires. Quite fulfilling to me, these desires have changed very little since I first wrote them. Meanwhile, they have functioned as a significant compass. As you seek and search out your calling, invite God to reveal the desires of your heart for your work, family, church, neighborhood, community, and world (Refer to the bottom of Diagram A).

Call to Work

Interestingly, the word "vocation" comes from the Latin word for call. What is your call to work? Perhaps you are a student or an engineer. Maybe you own a business or you manage a home or you do significant volunteer activity. Your present vocation is defined by how most of your time is spent. What are your heartfelt desires for work? As you engage in your work, what tasks and activities do you most enjoy? What do you least enjoy? Chances are good that your spiritual gifts are not active in the less enjoyable tasks. How about previous jobs—even when you were very young or employed in seemingly useless jobs?

As you might recall, for about eight years I was a biomedical engineer with the largest biomedical technology company in the world. With little job-searching effort, I am convinced that God gave me this position. You might say I was called to be an engineer. Though I have a science degree, I do not have an engineering degree. I began my biotechnology career through an internship arranged by Washington University, where I was to pursue an advanced degree. Later, I was offered a permanent position. My engineering career is a very wonderful story of God's gracious giving to me.

As an engineer, I found myself working beside some very dedicated people. One of them was Jim. Jim had a good sense of how his work was service to God and how he served God through his work. To Jim, they were one in the same. Jim was a very talented and innovative engineer. During one particular year, our company awarded him the highest technological honor for one of his inventions. Jim would probably say that his Lord inspired this innovation. God used this innovative biomedical technology to bring healing and wholeness to many. Jim enjoyed working on such innovations.

Jim's faith was not a showy faith. He did not talk about it all the time or even a great deal. He did not impose it on others. In fact, some probably did not know of Jim's beliefs. He treated all of his co-workers with the highest respect, care, and kindness. People would often go to Jim, seeking his counsel for their faith and lives. In my engineering department, several individuals credited Jim for renewing their trust in Jesus, positively affecting their whole lives. Many times Jim studied his Bible during the lunch hour. Yet he always was available to talk to whoever might interrupt his study time. One day a week, he led a Bible study during his lunch break. Perhaps the "teaching" or "shepherd" spiritual gifts were Jim's gifts. Jim carried this same approach into his family, church gathering, and community. Jim served Jesus in all areas of life.

Somehow Jim's approach rubbed off on me. I was not in any way a clone of Jim. In fact the two of us were quite different. I began to see God leading, guiding, and inspiring me with wisdom and creativity. Because I did not have an engineering degree like most others, many times I felt inadequate. Early on, I was asked to develop a device to accomplish a certain function. Previous attempts had been largely unsuccessful. I felt overwhelmed. I thought to myself, *How in the world am I going to think up such a concept especially if others couldn't do it?* Because I felt intimidated, I began to pray. One day I had this thought, *God is the Creator of the world. Surely God could solve this problem.* I asked God to show me a workable concept. A couple of weeks later, I suddenly had an idea. I knew that God had inspired this idea. It seemed workable.

There is more to the story, but I unexpectedly received a US patent for this invention. Later in a similar way, I was honored again with a couple more patents.

While an engineer, God used my spiritual gifts. Though I could not have named my spiritual gifts at the time, now I can look back and see them functioning. I enjoyed project management—taking a concept to market by putting together all the needed tasks, resources, and people for the process. Project management employed my spiritual gifts of administration and leadership. I designed new concepts with my wisdom and visionary-faith gifts. Exercising my leadership, administration, and teaching gifts, I was elected by my peers to a board that planned and executed continuing education events for technical employees. Using my teaching gift, I trained interns who worked under my boss's supervision. Employing my teaching and leadership gifts, I taught physicians about our products through presentations.

Until then, I had not shared much of my God experience with others. Though I did not look for opportunities, nonetheless God created occasions to share about my trust in Jesus. This was not an everyday experience. Still, quite miraculously over time, I did see several lives transformed.

Some years later when I was employed and doing ministry in a "church," I suddenly realized that I had been doing ministry all along even as an engineer. The biomedical company was tremendous training ground for what Martin Luther termed "ministry in daily life." In fact, simultaneously I was called to be an engineer and a minister.

"This is holy ground; I'm standing on holy ground. For the Lord is present and where he is … is holy." This simple song expresses it well. All of life is holy. God has declared and called us to be holy or sacred (Latin). The Lord through the Holy Spirit has taken up residence in you, me, and every other believer in Jesus. Therefore, the place where you are standing is holy or sacred ground. For the believer, the sacred and secular are not divided. Thus all of your life is sacred—not secular—because your life has been set apart for God's purposes. All of life is ministry or service to God. This is why "ministry in daily life" is such a powerful concept.

Later my call changed. Remember God's call is dynamic, shifting, and changing. I became primarily a stay-at-home mom, managing and making a home. Alongside of being a mom, I was called to serve as a part-time youth minister. Now very recently, I became an ordained pastor. Let me stress that as an ordained pastor, I am not any more significant to God than when I was an engineer or a stay-at-home mom, and certainly not any more significant than you. To God, everyone is equally valuable. Even if your actions seem small, they are very great in God's masterful plan.

Like my own vocation, your work may have several transitions. The famous job-hunting book *What Color Is Your Parachute* is a helpful manual for career changes. Quite frequently, youth, young adults, the suddenly unemployed, middle-aged people, and those about to retire are in times of transition. In the midst of mid-life restlessness, you may be asking: What am I going to do now that I've grown up? This question is the focus of Bob Buford's book *Halftime: Changing Your Game Plan from Success to Significance*.

What is your present vocation? What are your desires for work, both now and in the future? Where do you use your spiritual gifts? What do you most enjoy? Is it possible for you to shift less enjoyable responsibilities to someone else? What is your call to work?

Call to Family and Home

God calls you to thrive at home as well as at work. What is your call to family? What are your heartfelt desires for your marriage? What are your desires for your children? What are your desires for your home?

Twelve of my original heartfelt desires pertained to my home. Unedited from how I first hand-wrote them, these twelve describe my hopes for home and family:

1. A healthy, whole family with these dynamics: balance between individual and together time; secure, stable, and dependable environment; place of grace, caring, supportiveness, love of life, and fun; peaceful; relaxing; place to release burdens; place to learn and grow; place of faith and nourishment; refuge; safe (open to be myself); caring and nurturing; healthy giving.

2. Live as a family overseas. Take the kids to a cross-cultural place to experience the world.

3. Design and build our own home that is matched to our needs, values, and aesthetics (also energy efficient).

4. Build a community of families: sharing possessions; supporting one another in values and relationships.

5. Balanced and whole lifestyle: rest, healthy eating, exercise,

relaxation, leisure, solitude, spiritual growth, vocation, and healthy relationships (God, spouse, family and friends).

6. Creative homemaker: aesthetically beautiful (arts) and healthy environment (relational, emotional, spiritual environment), encouraging individuality, traditions and togetherness.

7. Pay ___ percentage (though not all) of kids' college education: not burdensome, yet encouraging responsibility and ownership.

8. Parenting dynamics and direction: love and care unconditionally; lead them to Lord Jesus; caregivers to kids—physically, emotionally, and spiritually (word, action, attitude, use of my time); teaching through words, action, example, values, guiding principles, functional skills (healthy communication skills, responsibility for self, care and respect for others); affirming and nurturing each child's unique talents, gifts, and interests; equip and release for life (function and live healthily); encourage love of God, self and neighbor; encourage trust of God; teach important life values (value of relationships, need vs. want, respect for creation).

9. Preserve past heritage: baby books, albums, video, scrapbooks, etc.

10. Financially support children.

11. Character traits: gratefulness, thankfulness, honesty, humility, respect for boundaries, affirmation, encouragement, confidence, trustworthy, faith-filled, love, joy, peace, patience, kindness, goodness, faithfulness, self-control.

12. Build a good marriage: realize our potential; encouragement; bear each others' burdens; relationship of rejoicing; understand one another; deep sharing; talk about and

accept our differences; stay "in love"; encourage absolute best; honesty without negativity.

As you review my heartfelt desires for home and family, you may not comprehend all of them. It is not necessary that you understand them since they are my desires, not yours. Over the years, they have shaped my call to family.

If you really know me, you will know that I have failed miserably at some of them. In fact, maybe with some, I have failed more times than I have succeeded. At least as written, a small few may never happen and that's okay. Some of these desires are very broad. However, over time, God has guided me to specific wisdom, making them more concrete. For example, Stephen Covey's "relationship bank account" and Sherod Miller's interpersonal communication skill-building course have impacted me quite a significantly. These people's expertise is applauded and recommended. Once again, I hope that fear has not invaded your being. I also hope that suddenly you do not have regrets. This is not my desire in the least. If so, focus ahead. Letting go of regrets will allow you to live more fully in your call—more on this later.

I am not suggesting that my heartfelt desires are ideal. I was a new mother when I wrote my heartfelt desires. Your family, home, and life circumstances are likely quite different. You may be young and single. You may be a single parent. You may not have children. You may be anticipating retirement. In any case, your heartfelt desires should reflect your unique circumstances.

If you are single and hope to be married, focus on your other heartfelt desires including those for work, church, neighborhood, community, and world. If you know your calling in these other arenas, you will find a greater measure of contentment—even if your desire for marriage does not come to fruition. Meanwhile, find other fulfilling ways to satisfy your desire for meaningful companionship.

Through the years, a lot of single people hoping for marriage have written their heartfelt desires for a spouse. What characteristics are desirable, important, or non-negotiable for you? Instead of getting caught up in physical attraction or romance while dating, you will be able to evaluate whether you can share a fulfilling relationship, and more importantly, a lifelong commitment with another person. Begin to pray for your future spouse. Even if your desire for marriage does not come to pass, being single and content far surpasses being unhappily married.

Many years ago, I recorded heartfelt desires for a future spouse and these were helpful as I dated. Graciously, God has given me a wonderful husband. If you are married, hopefully your spouse will be the primary human relationship in your life. One of my friends said, "The best way to love your kids is to love your spouse." The quality of your marriage will greatly influence all your other relationships. Because so many excellent marriage resources are available, we will not devote much space to marriage.

For me, my home and family are extremely important. Because this is true, for seventeen years I chose to be primarily a stay-at-home mom. For much of my life, the arenas of family and work have overlapped. Being a mom and managing a household was my primary vocation.

I am not asserting that staying home is ideal for all.

However, I am saying that I was quite content postponing some of my work desires because family was so important to me. In fact, becoming a pastor took twenty years, and I have no regrets about this length of time. The objective is not for you to copy me; instead, God longs to reveal your own unique heartfelt desires to you. One-size-fits-all is not possible for unique people.

Personal growth—counseling, spiritual director, other parental figures, significant friendships … learn and grow, healing of past hurts, to be a functional person, work on issues in my life.

I share this one additional desire because, especially with home and family, I have needed a lot of help. Let me repeat, *a lot* of help!

Throughout the years, the family of God has significantly supported me. We have many moms, dads, sisters, brothers, children, grandparents, and grandchildren. Relationships of depth and quality can be found in the extended family of God. The family of God has complemented and supplemented my blood family.

Because I have lived far from my biological parents, often parents in the family of God have encouraged me. Their wisdom has been a gift. Some have not known the role that they have played. Not coincidentally, many of these parental figures have a spiritual gift of encouragement.

One of my friends possesses much wisdom related to family and home. Quite without trying, she has taught me much about relationships. I joke with her that she is my family consultant. She was endowed with the "shepherd" gift. Another spiritual friend helps to lift and carry my burdens. For over twenty years, she faithfully has prayed daily for my family. Wow! What a treasure! By the way, she has the spiritual gift of intercession. She even prays for many of my friends whom she has not met. For years, I did not have a spiritual director. Now recently, my spiritual director carefully assists me in discerning God's activity in my life.

All families have weaknesses, including my own. As an added bonus, the family of God has complemented and supplemented my blood family in ways that have permitted me to graciously accept my blood family's weaknesses.

One of my pastoral professors said, "It is a sign of health, not weakness, to realize when you might need a professional counselor." In fact, because I highly respected this professor's wisdom, I listed counseling in this desire under personal growth. Many very healthy and highly functional people that I have known have sought the wisdom of a professional counselor. For a short time, the counselor helped them to navigate a challenging situation. To prepare for being a pastor, all students at my seminary were required to meet with a professional counselor at two different points in the preparation process. For me, the counselors' expertise was extremely helpful. One time, I acquired some important conflict-resolution skills. Somehow, you are not an inferior person for seeking professional help; rather, finding helpful wisdom results in strength and wholeness.

Finally, I have discovered an insight particularly helpful in my marriage. Let me first remind you that my husband is a great gift to me. Joel and I each have unique characteristics and gifts; therefore, we are different. Without intentionally thinking about them, they operate in our home and family. In the past, I wondered why Joel did not take a greater interest in planning and organization. Sometimes this was a source of frustration and conflict between us. One day the Spirit suddenly revealed an insight to me. Planning and organization fit my leadership and administration gifts, not his gifts. Therefore, these functions could be more naturally and effectively incorporated into my responsibilities rather than his tasks and duties. However, Joel has the "shepherd" and "encouragement" gifts; therefore, our children are more likely to have a heart-to-heart conversation with him than with me. Meanwhile, I relate to our children a bit differently. I might talk to them about their custom design and call. Embracing our differences was a helpful step forward for Joel and me.

Though you and your spouse may share much in common, each of you is also custom designed, and therefore, very different. Consider discussing with one another each of your unique gifts and attributes. This exercise will permit you to accept and even embrace many of your differences. You might realize that together you greatly complement and supplement one another. "Complement" is a helpful concept. It emphasizes the positive nature of our differences. Often these differences will cause two people (married or not) to have different approaches for a situation. By understanding your differences, you and another person will strengthen your relationship, increase your effectiveness, and even avoid frustration and conflict.

What are your heartfelt desires for your home, both now and in the future? What are your desires for marriage? What desires do you have for your children and parenting? How can the family of God support you? What is your call to family?

Call to Neighborhood, Community, and World

What are your heartfelt desires for your neighborhood, community, and world? Where could you use your uniqueness to be a transforming influence?

A lawyer once tested Jesus by inquiring how he might inherit eternal life. Jesus asked him what was written in the law. The lawyer had the right answer: "You shall love the Lord your God with all your heart, and with all your soul, and with all your strength, and with all your mind; and your neighbor as yourself."

"Do this and you will live," Jesus responded.

Wanting to justify himself, the lawyer further pressed Jesus, "Who is my neighbor?"

Jesus relayed a story about two very religious people who ignored a robbed and beaten man, passing him by on the other side of the road. Instead, a despised Samaritan rescued the injured man. Jesus asked, "Who was a *neighbor* to the wounded man?" (Luke 10:25–37, NRSV).

So, who is your neighbor down the street, in the community, or across the ocean? Your neighbor is whoever crosses your path. You are called to be a neighbor whether near or far, or out and about—at the school board meeting, in the Boy Scouts, or on a mission endeavor.

God may call you to a "neighborhood" where you normally would not live. For many years, some friends have chosen to live in a very poor and racially diverse neighborhood of their city. According to their financial means, they easily could live in suburbia. However, God has called them to break down cultural barriers, build friendships, and be neighborly in a new and different place.

God may call you to sacrifice on behalf of others. My own neighbor always is surprising people with her home-made cooking. During the short span of our friendship, several times she has been a neighbor to me, bringing me dinner for no apparent reason. Some other neighbors gave birth to quadruplets. For a whole year, she spent one night per week, rocking babies. She gave the gift of sleep to weary parents, while sacrificing her own. Meanwhile back home, her husband took charge of the household with their own young children. Having the "encouragement" and "shepherd" spiritual gifts, positive and giving describe this neighbor.

For still others, God may call you to be a neighbor across the ocean. Jim is a physician at a medical clinic near his home. Every few years for several months at a time, his family pays their own expense to travel and live in Kenya. Jim shares his medical skills at a hospital there while sacrificing his wages at home. Meanwhile Jim and his wife Brenda negotiate with their public school system to complete their children's requirements while absent. When at home, Brenda is transforming the neighborhood nearby. She directs a non-profit organization to encourage emotional, relational, and spiritual healing. Now some added perspective! Since Brenda was very young, she has suffered from very debilitating and painful rheumatoid arthritis. Knees, elbows, and hips—all these joints have been replaced. No! She is not a complainer. Her health handicaps do not hinder her neighborliness. If served the same lot in life, Kenyan adventures would not cross the minds of most. Rather than over here, God has called this family to a neighborhood over there, and they are fulfilled by their efforts.

Finally, are you called to be the mayor, city manager, police or fire chief? God has given a vision for our "city on a hill" to our own community leaders. Though these leaders do not ostentatiously display their trust in Jesus, it is deeply integrated into all their daily activities. Not only civic leaders, but also faithful business and education leaders are transforming our city. Weekly, these citizens pray for their community.

Who are your neighbors day by day? Where could you meaningfully use your gifts in your neighborhood or community, and world? What are your heartfelt desires for transforming our world? How are you called to be a neighbor?

Church: The Called-Out Ones

My husband and I have uncovered a great discovery. Church in the biblical Greek literally translated means called-out ones. We concluded that call is very central to "being" and "doing" church. For years, our own church gatherings have custom designed around the unique calls of people, the called-out ones. (Ephesians 4:15–16)

God is calling you, and therefore, you are one of the called-out ones. You are the church. You are called to be the church twenty-four hours a day and seven days a week. You are an important member in your gathering of the called-out ones.

What are your heartfelt desires for your church, the "called-out ones" of Jesus Christ? What is your role or function in the called-out ones? What is your call?

God called some from my church to plant personal vision in

young people through retreats. This retreat ministry was not a program copied from some other church gathering. With other young adults, I planned, organized, and taught workshops for youth in high school and college. Though unidentified at the time, I used my gifts of teaching, administration, and leadership. Our work was very meaningful. We were called to be "ministers." We were called to the priesthood of all believers. You and all other believers are called to the same (1 Peter 2:4–9).

Neither the pastors nor the leadership body controlled this ministry. Instead "lay people" financially supported and operated this ministry. "Lay" comes from the biblical Greek word for people—ordinary everyday people. "Lay person" suggests a false hierarchy and value differential. When I served on these retreats, simultaneously God called me to be an engineer. Later God called me to be an ordained pastor. Back then and now, I have always been a lay person—an ordinary, everyday person like anyone else.

Although my church gathering was clearly focused upon the Gospel of Jesus, it was very unique from other church gatherings. Besides the pastors and other staff, there was a vast army of church workers serving Jesus both inside and outside the walls of the building. There was a counseling center, free and open to the public. While also owning a private practice, a professional counselor directed this counseling center, giving his time as an offering to God. A "lay" woman began a prayer ministry with overnight retreats, teaching people to recognize God's guidance. About ten very well attended spiritual growth classes were offered for adults. Oftentimes without a published curriculum, these scriptural classes were designed, prepared, and taught not only by pastors, but many "lay" people. During worship, "lay" people prayed with individuals, lifting their cares and concerns to our God. Others led marriage classes. Still others were trained to visit people in the hospital or at home. At one time, our church gathering supported and sent out over fifty of our own people as world missionaries.

Here is the miracle. My church gathering began small and continued with a few hundred people for many years. Then for still more years, it really was not much bigger. Meanwhile, the pastor and other leaders were constantly seeking our Lord while teaching and training people.

Why? Jesus called the original twelve disciples to know and follow him. In turn, Jesus trained them to serve by demonstrating true service with his life. Finally, Jesus sent them out to do the same. The Holy Spirit came upon them, empowering them and all believers with spiritual gifts to continue what he began.

In like manner, my pastor called us to be Jesus' disciples—to know, follow, and serve him. We came to know Jesus through prayer and God's Word. We discovered that the Holy Spirit empowers us with spiritual gifts in order to uniquely serve in daily life. Everyone was encouraged to know their ministry.

More and still more people were serving Jesus in unique and significant ways. God's work was multiplied. Yes! The pastors had their roles. I wondered: If everyone knew their custom design and call, what could a multitude accomplish for God?

When you believed and were baptized, you were filled with God's Spirit. You were empowered to be a minister. "Service" and "ministry" are translated from the same word in the biblical Greek. Somehow, ministry is reserved for pastors and staff people. In turn, service is for all others, suggesting something lesser. Service means pitching in. Most likely, pitching in is not very fun, and even may be drudgery.

Over eight years, I saw *God* multiply our church gathering from about eight hundred individuals to over twenty-five hundred people. Keep in mind that for many more years, this church gathering was much smaller. My pastor later acknowledged that *God* surprised him with such growth. Yeah! Rather than people attempting to plan and engineer expansion, "*God* added to their number" (Acts 2:47). *God* was clearly in charge. Quite often, sinful people pursue and take the credit for numbers; therefore, I hesitate to inform you of this growth.

Rather than numbers, this church gathering emphasized God and people. They did not emphasize any particular organizational structure, such as committees or some organizational hierarchy. Nor did they emphasize finding ideas and programs. Occasionally though, God did call some people to do a program or class used elsewhere. Neither did they emphasize the facility. In fact, often the facility was over crowded; however, people did not stay away—quite the opposite in fact. Though financial challenges were experienced, my church gathering seemed to be always optimistic about God's provision. Even though I was very active for several years, I never heard about the budget, and there were no pledge drives. Instead my church's teachers taught me about God's provision, tithing, the wise management of resources, and how these scriptural principles could set me free. Without a doubt, my view of this church gathering is probably overly pristine. Behind the scenes, there was no doubt struggle, conflict, and confusion.

Now, my goal is not to make smaller church gatherings

into larger gatherings. Maybe *God* desires for some church gatherings to remain small. Rather, I am about growing the kingdom of God—God's rule and reign on earth, and in people's lives. I am not about maintaining or growing an institution or organization that we label "church." In fact, throughout church history, God has allowed institutions labeled as "church" to die.

Instead, my desire is for you to say, "I am the church. I am the church all the time—at home, at work and out in the community. We are the church. You and I are the called-out ones. God is calling me and I am invigorated by God's call to me. God is calling me to be a disciple—to know, follow, and serve Jesus. I am called to be a member and to have a particular function in the body of Christ—God's church."

What are your heartfelt desires for your church gathering? What would you like your role or function to be? How could your custom design best be used for God's work? If you do many things in your church gathering, what would you like to stop doing in order to invest your time differently?

For many years, God has called my husband and me to serve as pastors and leaders of the "called-out ones." Remember "church" is literally translated "called-out ones." God has called us to teach the "called-out ones" about their call. Our Lord has taught us how to custom design our gathering of the "called-out ones" around the calls of people while laying aside all of our preconceived plans, ideas, and notions of what each of the "called-out ones" is called to be and do.

If "I am the church," then "I am the church" wherever I go and whatever I do. You also are the church twenty-four hours a day and seven days a week as shown on Diagram C. In other words, you are the domestic church in your family. At work, you are the vocational church. While at the grocery store or somewhere else in your neighborhood or community, you are the out-and-about church. Finally, you are the gathered church when you come together with others to hear good news, be encouraged, and worship your God. Maybe rather than compelling you to be involved "at church," the gathered church should propel you to live a life worthy of the call in your work, family, neighborhood, community, and world—to be the true "you" that our Lord has custom designed you to be.

What am I *Called* to do?

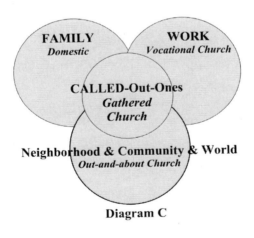

Diagram C

Jesus said, "I came that they may have life, and have it abundantly" (John 10:10, NRSV).

Called to the Greatest Relationship

First things first. In order for you to truly understand your call, there is something more basic and fundamental for you to know and experience.

Once, I was particularly challenged by some faith questions. As a result, I went and talked with a pastor friend. He said, "I can tell that you are a person who wants to love and serve God. So don't worry so much about these questions. Don't even think about them. Instead, make it your number-one goal in life to know Jesus and then all else will fall into place." Simplistic? Perhaps! However, I have found it to be the best advice that I have ever received, and I have returned to this wisdom over and over again. Even now when life gets confusing or I am hurting or I feel like I have lost my way or I am having a hard time with some circumstance in my life, God will shift my attention to this simple advice: *Make it your number-one goal in life to know Jesus and then all else will fall into place.* I have a relationship with God's son Jesus, a relationship characterized by forgiveness, love, trust, and wholeness. This relationship is all that I need for life.

You are called to the greatest relationship. When I once reflected upon every "call" scripture, I discovered God's call could be summarized by a few words: You are called to know, follow, and uniquely serve Jesus. This relationship is essential and indispensable. It is the best and most-profound relationship. Through knowing, following, and serving Jesus, you will integrate all your insights and put the pieces together. You will even answer those two life-defining questions. You will find wisdom and guidance, experience joy, know deep love, discover the meaning of life, receive healing, and be the kind of person that most people would want to be. Knowing, following, and serving Jesus is putting first things first.

Call to *Know* Jesus Deeply and Personally

God the Father sent his Son in a person named Jesus. The invisible God became a visible human being. God can be known best through a friendship with Jesus (John 17:3). Knowing Jesus is foundational.

"Know" is a curious word. You may know a fair amount about a famous person, but unless you become personally acquainted, you will never know this person as a friend. This may be true of Jesus as well. You might know a lot *about* Jesus, but not really know Jesus—at least not very well.

The biblical Greek word *koinonia* describes relationships where people know each other well. From *koinonia* (often translated *fellowship*), we get our English words common, community, and communion. *Koinonia* describes relationships of great depth where people mutually share their lives with one another. They share their time, thoughts, feelings, burdens, insecurities, joys, brokenness, and sometimes even their possessions. I deeply desire human relationships of this kind. However, the greatest and most complete *koinonia* relationship possible is with God's Son, Jesus, and you are called to a *koininia* relationship with him (1 Corinthians 1:9).

Relationship with Jesus far surpasses the very best human friendship and even the perfect marriage. Friendship is not a one-time happening. Rather, friendship must be continually renewed. Like any friendship, I can know Jesus, and still, I can know him better. In fact, the Old Testament uses Hebrew words reserved for the most intimate relationships to describe this kind of knowing. Many years ago when I struggled with those two key questions, I did know Jesus. I longed for my life to reflect these words: "For to me, to live is Christ" (Philippians 1:21, NIV). Somehow, through knowing Jesus better and better, I even found answers for my questions.

When you deeply know and love someone, you want to spend time together. You want to talk and listen to one another. You want to know the ways of your friend. Your outlook and character are shaped by this friendship. You want to spend time with others who also know this one. You want to eat together. You want to speak highly of your friend with others.

When I worship, I am in the presence of my friend. I praise him for what he means to me and thank him for his friendship. I carry on a conversation with my friend through prayer. Jesus lovingly talks to me through his written words recorded in the Scriptures (Hebrews 4:12–16). He converses with me in other ways as well. Jesus helps me to figure out life (2 Timothy 3:16–17). I eat bread and wine with Jesus' friends. Always, I am reminded that this friend loved me so much that he sacrificed his life for me. My friend always forgives my sins. I know that I am deeply loved. Without this relationship, all of these actions would be mere religious ritual.

In fact, I have been adopted into Jesus' family. Like Jesus, I am a beloved child of the Father. Because I am a daughter, I am an heir. I have already inherited all the riches and blessings of this family. These blessings include the provision of all good things: material resources, healing care, friends, spiritual gifts, talents and skills, a future, hope, and a significant place in the family plan. I get surprised and overwhelmed by all of these meaningful gifts. As a beloved child, I keep receiving endless gifts over and over again. In fact, everything is a gift. Grace is what I call this endless giving (1 Corinthians 15:10). You also are called to know Jesus and this endless grace is available to you.

Call to *Follow* Jesus in All of Your Life

When you know Jesus and are surrounded by his love and grace, quite naturally you will begin to trust him and even follow him. Richard Nelson Bolles shares a helpful image:

Imagine yourself out walking in your neighborhood one night, and suddenly you find yourself surrounded by such a dense fog, that you have lost your bearings and cannot find your way. Suddenly, a friend appears out of the fog, and asks you to put your hand in theirs, and they will lead you home. And you, not being able to tell where you are going, trustingly follow them, even though you can only see one step at a time. Eventually you arrive safely home, filled with gratitude. But as you reflect upon the experience the next day, you realize how unsettling it was to have to keep walking when you could see only one step at a time, even though you had guidance in which you knew you could trust.[1]

Life can be a lot like this foggy road. Therefore, I need someone who loves and cares about me to lead me step by step by step. When Jesus is my greatest friend, I will want nothing else but to trust and follow him. Perhaps this last statement is very difficult for you to believe. If so, then take the advice of my friend, "Don't even think about this! Instead, make it your number one goal in life to know Jesus, and then all else will fall into place." Do not read any further. This goal will be sufficient. If, however, you have tasted that Jesus is all about leading you and giving to you all that you need to live, then continue on.

Follow may be a scary word for you because of what it implies. I am convinced that fear is often the greatest hurdle to following Jesus. We fear that Jesus will lead us somewhere we would never want to go. We fear the unknown. We fear that Jesus is going to deal us a royal bummer. We fear that Jesus is going to make us give up the one or two things that we love the most. We fear that we will turn into a person that we would never want to be. We fear that life will become dull and boring and certainly not any fun. We fear that we will have to live in something akin to poverty, having very little in the way of possessions. We fear that Jesus is going to make us do the one thing that we would never want to do—maybe go to Oogabooga land—and of course, that would be the most miserable experience. Forget it! Remember that image of the foggy road. Jesus is your loving friend—in fact, your greatest friend. Jesus is not about inspiring fear (2 Timothy 1:7). Rather, Jesus tells you over and over, "Do not be afraid" (John 14:27, Matthew 28:5, 10).

In order for you to trust and follow Jesus, the truth needs to be clear. It needs to sink deep into your heart and into your being. Jesus deeply loves you. Jesus was present at the beginning of creation, and he was present when you were custom designed. He knows every detail about you and every other person and if that is not enough, the whole world. Jesus is utterly brilliant. His Spirit—God's Holy Spirit—is living in you right now. Therefore he can lead you and guide you. When you truly know Jesus, he is not like any human person you may know. Jesus is not a hard taskmaster. Jesus is not about harsh criticism. Jesus is not a robber, longing to steal from you. Jesus is not about planting fear in your heart. Neither is Jesus a vending machine, producing upon demand all the things that you are sure that you need at any given point in time.

Jesus is the way (John 14:6). Learn from him. Listen to him. Let go and follow him. You will experience profound love. You will receive endless grace. You will be set free (John 8:31–32). You will know and pursue God's agenda. In his well-known book *Celebration of Discipline*, Richard Foster teaches us many life-giving practices used by Jesus and other faithful people through the centuries. They will help you to learn, listen, and let go. Many of these disciplines are applied throughout this book as well. You will not earn Jesus' love and favor by doing these practices. You already are blessed with all of his love, favor, and gifts. Rather through learning, listening, and letting go, you will come to know, trust and be led by the living Jesus in a still deeper way.

Bob Buford was at a crossroads in his life, seeking direction. He sought help from a strategic planning consultant. The planner who was an atheist asked him:

"What's in the box?"

By this, the planner was inquiring:

"What is the one thing that is the mainspring of your life?"

The planning consultant thought that Buford's "mainspring" was either Jesus or money. Choosing Jesus represented an act of faith for Buford. But even more, he relates:

> "It was a commitment to do something about the faith I already had. By acknowledging Christ as my guiding light, I had invoked the promise that he would direct my paths, no matter where they took me."

For Buford, putting Jesus alone in the box illustrated some of the great "paradoxes" of the faith:

> "To put Christ in the box is to break down the walls of the box and allow the power and grace of his life to invade every aspect of your own life. It follows the same wonderfully inverted logic as the ancient assertion that

> it is in giving that one receives, in our weakness we are
> made strong, and in dying we are born to richer life."[2]

Unbelievably, the *greatest freedom* (Galatians 5:13) comes from this kind of death (Luke 9:23–25). It is a death to thinking that I am capable of living apart from Jesus in the least little way. With this kind of death, I can know a confidence and hope that Jesus can take better care of me than I can take care of myself.

In fact, the longer that I know and follow Jesus, the more I realize how desperately I need him and how I could never get along without him.

You may not like the word sin. In fact, I really do not like it either. It puts me in touch with all of the things that I really do not like about myself. I would like to think that I never lied to anyone or never hurt anyone—at least not very seriously. I really am not all that bad, at least in comparison to that person over there (Luke 18:9–14). Therefore, I really do pretty well at following my friend Jesus' standards, ways, and intentions.

If I am truly honest, I am only trying to fool others and myself. My failures and wrongs disrupt and even destroy my relationship with Jesus and with others. They create a dividing wall. We all have felt the alienation of a diving wall, resulting from a broken relationship. I do not know about you, but I need to have this dividing wall removed and I need the resulting freedom. The good news is that my friend Jesus is forever chasing after me, constantly pursuing me while offering me total and complete forgiveness of all my wrongs and failures.

He is pursuing you also. Jesus forgave all your sins, past present and future, by dying on a cross. He removes the dividing wall. This forgiveness is freely given to you at no cost and with no requirement from you. This friendship is available to all who desperately know they need such a friend. Yes! It is possible to truly know Jesus in an incredibly intimate and personal relationship, characterized by humble honesty, mutual understanding, forgiveness, healing, and his free and gracious gifts. When you know Jesus, you do not suddenly become perfect, but rather now your sins, failures, and your very life are totally wrapped up in him. What I am describing is similar to a marriage. Your life and Jesus' life cannot be separated (Galatians 2:19–20, Ephesians 5:25–32).

At this point, if you are unsure or you do not like something about knowing and following Jesus, I say to you, "Don't worry!" Jesus will not stop calling you and offering the goodness of his friendship to you (Luke 15:3–10).

In fact, Jesus' call is like a constantly ringing telephone. Jesus is always calling you, always beckoning you, never forcing you, but continually trying to get your attention, constantly trying to reach out to you, and always wanting a friendship with you. Jesus is constantly trying to get your attention even when you are totally uninterested. Jesus is continually calling and constantly present in your life whether or not you choose to acknowledge or respond to his call. Everyday for a long time, Jesus has been calling ordinary people like you, not just religious leaders like pastors or missionaries. Jesus loves you so much that he does not force you to "answer" his call. If you really think about this constantly ringing phone, you will realize that first and foremost, Jesus has been, is presently, and forever will be pursuing and calling you. As a result, I am sure that you have already sensed Jesus' call to you.

Too often, I am easily diverted and distracted. However,

Jesus' presence, love, and care for me are uninterrupted, creating a very one-sided relationship at times. Off in the future, I am looking forward to a continuous and steadfast, and even eternal and everlasting friendship with Jesus (John 17:3). Sometimes I get a taste of this, and I hunger for it more and more. I hope you desire the same.

Call to Uniquely *Serve* Jesus

When you *know* Jesus and are captured by his love, you will want nothing else than to trust and *follow* him. As you follow Jesus, you will quite naturally but really supernaturally begin to *serve* him in all of your life. You will begin to clearly see and know how you are custom designed—who you are and what you are to do.

Thus *know, follow,* and *serve* describe a progression. It is not a progression of time. For when you are called to know Jesus, you are at the same time called to follow and serve Jesus. Often I use the image of a house to illustrate this progression. Knowing Jesus is like laying the foundation of the house. Following Jesus is like building the walls of the house. In turn, serving Jesus is what makes the house unique or custom designed in a multitude of ways. Like the foundation of a house, the call to know Jesus is essential. A house built without a foundation or walls is going to collapse. In like manner, if your serving does not result from knowing and following Jesus, it will be meaningless. To the original disciples, Jesus spoke this basic truth when he likened "building your life" to "building a house." Coming to Jesus, hearing his words and putting them into practice—it's like building a house upon a rock, and when the storms of life come, it will not fall because it is well built. (Matthew 7:24–27).

When I was a student, I greatly respected a certain older professor. He was truly a saint and a man full of the Spirit. He was a man of humble character, and he carefully chose his words. He knew and deeply loved Jesus. He genuinely cared about people. He loved and respected God's word. Referencing the following passage, he would scribble on my assignments: "Press On!"

"Yet whatever gains I had, these I have come to regard as loss because of Christ. More than that, I regard everything as loss because of the surpassing value of knowing Christ Jesus my Lord. I want to know Christ... Not that I have already obtained this... but I press on to make it my own... I press on toward the goal for the prize of the heavenly call of God in Christ Jesus" (Philippians 3:7–16, NRSV).

Called to Inspiration

God was not in the wind, earthquake, or fire for Elijah. Rather God spoke to him in a "gentle whisper," sometimes translated "still small voice" or "sheer silence" (1 Kings 19:11–16). In many and various ways throughout time, God has spoken—even in an audible voice to a very small few. God's call must be heard, and the key to hearing is listening. You might say this entire volume is about ways to listen for God's personal voice and promptings.

Many years ago, like many young parents, one day I was feeling a bit overwhelmed and insecure in my new parenting role. While reflecting upon some of Jesus' words that assured me of his care and encouraged me not to worry (Luke 12:22–32), the Spirit inspired a thought in me: *If you honestly recognize your wrongs and then specifically acknowledge them, humbly asking for forgiveness from your children, then your relationship with your children will be fine.* I suddenly felt reassured and filled with deep peace. In fact, I have applied this wisdom to all other relationships.

As you seek to know, follow, and serve the living Jesus, he will guide you by speaking to you and helping you to see ahead. Jesus' Spirit has taken up residence in you. You are called to be a temple of his Spirit (1 Corinthians 6:19). As a result, Jesus through the Spirit will direct you, speaking to you through his Word and prayer, particularly meditative prayer. Remember prayer is a conversation, both talking and listening. Jesus' Spirit inside of you will gently whisper to you, inspiring your thoughts, and using the still small voice inside of you. Jesus' Spirit might prompt a strong conviction, a clear inward impression, a deep motivation or desire, intense thought, excitement about pursuing something, a deep knowing, a feeling of being drawn to something, or a waterfall of new thoughts and ideas that make total sense—ideas that you will be personally and intimately involved in making happen. Jesus' indwelling Spirit always invents truly innovative and creative thoughts. Learn to listen and Jesus' Spirit will spontaneously inspire creativity in you.

Receiving Guidance and Vision

If children are taught and nurtured, even they can receive guidance through our Lord's Word and gentle whisper. At a relatively young age, I was privileged to learn many and various time-tested ways to receive direction and vision. Sometimes, I felt worried or challenged about some situation. I still feel this way at times. Often I would read my Bible until I felt differently about the circumstance. Sometimes a specific scripture passage would invade my thoughts. Other times, I might use a concordance to locate particular verses with a certain word such as anxious or encouragement. Always my Lord would transform me, changing my outlook, stimulating hope or showing me some new action to undertake. As a result of repeatedly returning to various passages, quite without trying, I committed to memory many passages from our Lord's Word. Sometimes at a needed moment, the Spirit would bring one of these learned passages to mind. Through personal experience, I discovered that God's Word is living and active, often transforming me without my even realizing it (Isaiah 55:10–11, Hebrews 4:12–16). Thus, God's Word has become an indispensable, irreplaceable, and personal guidebook for me.

While young, similar to Solomon in the Old Testament, I sought wisdom from God. If a circumstance puzzled me, I would ask for wisdom, expecting it to come. Almost always when I least expected it, the needed wisdom would come. Through a strong thought, God answered my request. The wisdom was like a key that opened the lock—seemingly the perfect answer.

Without a doubt, my God met me in my child-like expectancy. Now after many years of seeking and searching for my Lord's guidance, his Spirit has inspired all of these: encouragement, practical wisdom, specific direction, new insight, rest, revelation, vision, comfort, inspiration, an attitude adjustment, trust, peace, a deep experience of God's love, healing, release, creativity, greater understanding, a change of heart, grace, satisfaction of inner hunger, confidence, dissolved fears, joy, patience, kindness, goodness, faithfulness, self-control, surrender, a change of character, and true freedom. Much more could be added.

God's Gentle Whisper

Hearing God's gentle whisper is very exciting. It always has a definite sense of being initiated by God. I say to myself, *Wow! I did not make that up.* Amazingly, God's whisper always seems to be *gentle*, no matter what God whispers to me.

While in college, I began keeping a prayer journal. I never dreamed that I would still be at it many years later. My own journal was not a list of prayer concerns, though this is a common type of prayer journal. In the early days, I wrote letters to my Lord, expressing my thoughts, feelings, concerns, joys, blessings, worries, cares, concerns, or desires. I might describe a difficult situation or circumstance. I might record how Jesus had encouraged me. Many times, I confessed my failures and wrongs, seeking Jesus' mercy and forgiveness. I wrote expecting God to read all that I recorded.

Often, I would wait for God to compose a letter to me. I would write *Dear Wendy…,* and then low and behold, a whole stream of first person thoughts would be inspired in me, like the following: *I love you, my child. You are precious to me. I am working through this circumstance. Wait for me to work in this situation.* God has spoken many and various personal words to me. Most of the time now, I do not compose letters. Rather I use shorthand, sometimes jotting a few words or thoughts. Spiritual journaling is one of the many time-tested practices through which God may whisper to you.

Preparation for Hearing God's Gentle Whisper

Here in the USA, the phrase "very busy" fills the air far too frequently. In contrast, while traveling in Africa, I never recall hearing this expression. Though many people were physically very poor, they certainly were a lot less stressed and impatient. Emotionally and relationally, they were richer.

In this busy world, in order to actually hear God speak, you need to turn off the noise. Once when feeling really frenzied at work, I went to the lounge with my Bible in hand and sat for a moment or two. Calming thoughts from scripture eclipsed the chaos while my Lord invited me: "Cease striving and know that I am God" (Psalm 46:10a, NASB).

In order to prepare for listening, you need to quiet your mind, emotions, and whatever else needs to be calmed. The following preparation exercise is not meant to be a rigid step-by-step process. Improvise, allowing for theme and variation. Reflect, using your imagination.

1. Surrender all anxiety, tension, and troublesome emotions. Give these to your heavenly Father.

2. Surrender control of your life. If you have trouble, picture Jesus on the cross before you and put your focus there.

3. Surrender all of your cares and worries. Place these one by one into a box. Then hand the box to your heavenly Father.

4. Surrender all your good intentions. Instead Jesus will give you his good intentions.

5. Surrender your sin, wrongs, and failures, confessing them and turning from them. Receive Jesus' unending forgiveness given and accomplished for you when Jesus died on the cross and rose to new life.

Consider combining your reflection with journaling like me. Rather than attempting to hide your true thoughts, concerns, and feelings, recording them will compel you to reveal them to God. For me, transparency has propelled me to Jesus' profound mercy and grace over and over again. (Hebrews 4:12–16).

Vehicles for Hearing God's Gentle Whisper

"Praying the Scriptures" and "*lectio divina*" (translated divine reading) are ancient forms of meditation. This type of meditative prayer can be practiced in many and various ways. Over and over again, God has spoken to me through listening in this manner.

1. Begin by filling your mind with God's Word. Choose a shorter passage of Scripture, perhaps a few words or a verse.
2. Thank God for being with you. Invite God to speak to you. In your mind, picture Jesus there with you.
3. Read the words very slowly, perhaps one word at a time. Stay with each word until you believe God is moving you to the next word. You might stay with one word the entire time.
4. Pay attention to your thoughts as you move from word to word. This may be God speaking to you, perhaps guiding, healing, or teaching you.
5. Talk to Jesus as you read, perhaps praying the very words of the Scripture passage.
6. Consider jotting down your thoughts: a word, two to three

sentences or whatever seems appropriate. Maybe write a poem or prayer, draw, paint or use some other creative expression.

7. Respond to God. Thank God for speaking to you or whatever comes from your heart.

8. If needed, talk about your experience with a respected and trusted Christian friend.

Remember receiving God's guidance is not about your agenda. In this production minded culture, it is not about quantity, but rather depth and quality.

Practicing the Presence of God

Practicing the presence of God is ideal for busy people. Mix it up with all the minutes and activities of your day. Move in joyful awareness of God's presence with whispered prayers of praise and adoration flowing continuously from your heart. Brother Lawrence, a monk of the historical church, penned a classic illuminating this concept:

> *... the time of business does not with me differ from the time of prayer; and in the noise and clatter of my kitchen, while several persons are at the same time calling for different things, I possess God in as great a tranquility as if I were upon my knees at the blessed sacrament.*[1]

Simple breath prayers like the well-known "Jesus prayer" can cultivate this practice. Using the rhythm of your breathing, pray over and over, "Lord Jesus Christ, Son of God, have mercy on me, a sinner." I use this prayer when I am feeling scattered. To add more meaning to this prayer, slowly and reflectively review one of the scripture passages where this prayer originates (Luke 18:9–14). Reflect upon the characters in the passage. Which character most resembles you? One of them desperately sees his need for God's mercy. Too often I am like the blind Pharisee.

Since she was young, my friend has murmured the Jesus prayer and numerous other simple breath prayers. For her, the pause at a red stoplight triggers a breath prayer. Praising her Lord, she might say, "For God is (great, good, etc) and his (mercy, grace, etc) endures forever. Praise be to God."

Richard Foster offers insight for discovering a simple breath prayer:

> *Find some uninterrupted time and a quiet place and sit in silence, being held in God's loving presence. After a few moments allow God to call you by name: "Christy," "Nathan," "Joel," "Tess," "Carolynn," "Richard," "Lynda," "Joy." Next, allow this question to surface: "What do you want?" Answer this question simply and directly. Maybe a single word will come to your conscious mind: "peace," "faith," "strength." Perhaps it will be a phrase: "to understand your truth," "to feel your love." Next, connect this phrase with the most comfortable way you have of speaking about God: "blessed Savior," "Abba," "Immanuel," "Holy Father," "gracious Lord." Finally, you will want to write out your breath prayer, staying within what is comfortable to say in one breath.*[2]

Practicing the presence of God will facilitate unceasing conversation with our Lord (1 Thessalonians 5:17). Wouldn't it be wonderful to always be connected with your God? As you engage in these practices, let freedom and creativity be your companions, remembering that God personally speaks to us in all sorts of ways. Expect various seasons. Days of desert, distraction, and even detour will suddenly give way to a lofty mountaintop experience.

Creating Time and Space

Real silence and solitude with the absence of ringing phones, computers, or people talking to you—either for many minutes, several hours or even days—can enhance your ability to recognize God's voice and movement in your life.

Creating intentional time for listening and being alone with God is a top priority for me. Listening for God is a great "get to do it," not a "have to do it" activity. For me, it is life sustaining and addicting. Divine addiction is healthy and beneficial.

Begin small—perhaps five minutes at a time. For most people, watching a little less TV would create time for listening to God. Spending time with the almighty God who can do great things in your life or watching some TV show—which do you believe will yield the best result? Maybe you will have an almost daily time in the morning or evening. Since I am not a morning person, I try to spend time with God during the first available time in my day not requiring my attention for something necessary. At times, I particularly enjoy listening during the night watch, relaxing in the quiet stillness of my living room with the peaceful darkness outside my window. If a daily time is challenging, schedule a longer period of time that occurs more sporadically. Perhaps a Saturday morning or

Sunday afternoon might accommodate you. If you travel a fair amount, set aside the time spent on an airplane. Try scheduling a retreat. Maybe you will have a get-away place that facilitates your listening. I strongly encourage you to find a way for these valuable and vital God encounters.

Remember this time will not be wasted and unproductive. Rather it will be the opposite. For me, efficiency and productivity have increased because I am less distracted, and even have received time saving insights while listening. As you start to recognize God's voice during these intentional times, then you will be attentive to it at other times as well. Once as I stood in the darkness by an ocean shore with large waves crashing near me, unexpectedly my Lord whispered to me, "This is what my steadfast love is like—relentless and continuous."

True Guidance and Vision

Clear vision requires listening. Listening and seeing are intimately related to one another.

Today, the word *vision* can be used in ways that are very disconnected from a living God. We even may think that vision comes from people sitting around "at church," manufacturing all kinds of ideas. However, this is not necessarily true spiritual vision. God's vision is so beyond our minute imaginations.

Jesus emphasized the importance of recognizing his voice of guidance and distinguishing it from other voices (John 10:1–6). True guidance and vision begin and end with God's Word. Our Lord's direction will never conflict with his Word. Because God has worked so powerfully in my life through the Word, the Scriptures have quite naturally become a check and balance, protecting me from harmful behavior and from zooming off in the wrong direction. I hope that they will be an authority for you as well.

God-given vision is the opposite of spiritual blindness. Many biblical Greek words have to do with spiritual vision: revelation, enlighten, manifestation, appear, light and even the biblical Greek word translated "know" literally means "has come to see." This biblical Greek word, *know* is similar to our English word, insight or inner sight.

The most basic form of vision is for you to clearly "see" Jesus as a full revelation of God. You need to "see" who Jesus is, why he came to earth, and what he came to do. You need to "see" your desperate need for his death on the cross and his resurrection, allowing you to receive a whole new life. Finally you personally need to "come to see" and know Jesus in a very deep and intimate way. To clearly know someone and their desires, listening is imperative. Nothing can be more exciting and compelling than hearing Jesus' call and seeing with his vision as you know and follow him (Galatians 1:15–16).

God-given vision is an ability to clearly see and understand the past, present, and also God's desires for the future. God-given vision is like a picture or road map, leading us into the future while bestowing the accompanying faith to believe that this vision will become reality.

How and where do you find the answers to those two key questions? God has custom designed *you*, and is all about calling *you*, personally speaking to *you*, guiding *you*, and giving vision to *you*. In the midst of it all, our Lord will always be right on time, sometimes early, but never late.

"I keep asking that the God of our Lord Jesus Christ, the glorious Father, may give you the Spirit of wisdom and revelation, so that you may know him better. I pray also that the eyes of your heart may be enlightened in order that you may know the hope to which he has called you, the riches of his glorious inheritance in the saints, and his incomparably great power for us who believe." (Ephesians 1:17–19a, NIV).

Called to Support and Trust

Individuality does not imply individualism. God did not call us to be lone rangers, but rather our Lord created us for relationships of support and trust. Jesus promised that where two or three gather in his name, there he would be also (Matthew 18:20).

My faithful family and trusted friends have encouraged and confirmed my call to create this book. For years, some of them have labored alongside of me, discovering its message—even though at the time, none of us really knew that we were writing a book. We felt called to our work together. We had a strong sense that our God was guiding and leading us. Through our endeavors, we truly saw our Lord accomplish incredible deeds. In the midst of our common efforts, we became close friends.

Maybe it was the other way around. In the midst of becoming close friends, we really liked working together, or maybe some of both. It is not as if we always agreed or we never hurt one another, but in the midst of it all, without even realizing it we were experiencing God's incredible love. We became both givers and receivers of our Lord's rich blessings.

God will provide trustworthy and caring people to encourage, support, and labor with you as well. They will prod you to persevere and stay focused. They also will function as a check and balance so that you will not get off track and distracted. God will use these people to confirm your calling.

To identify your trusted friends and family members, contemplate these characteristics. Who have been genuine and loyal cheerleaders in your life? Who do you deeply respect for their practical insight and wisdom, especially spiritual insight and wisdom? Name those to whom you could bare your soul, revealing your true thoughts and feelings. Who does or might pray for you consistently and regularly? List those who encourage you to grow in a loving, non-threatening, affirming, and even healing manner. Reflect upon whom you feel very comfortable asking for feedback and advice.

For me, my husband Joel is invaluable. He believes in me—who I am and what I do. My best bud, Julie, sustained me while growing up. My friends, Toni and Steve, cheered me on through my twenty-year process to become a pastor. Right now, both Steve(s) and Edsel encourage me in my "call" passion. Presently my spiritual director, Liz, and some of my praying friends, offer profound insight and wisdom. Their wise advice is a treasure. Right now, I could reveal almost anything to Linda and the Penn house gang. Linda,

Harriette, and Kathy bless me with their constant prayers along with my friends in the Tuesday morning prayer group as well as many in my church gathering. Throughout my life, a multitude of friends and family have supported me, loving and caring for me. Thank you!

Good spiritual companions deserve and uphold the labels of trust and respect. First, these people likely care for you. Over time you have built a bond of trust. Further, they are respected for their devout faith, remarkable wisdom, upright character, and profound knowledge of you. A good spiritual friend will know the quality of your faith. They will be prayerful and have an understanding of the Scriptures as well. This insight and familiarity with both you and God's Word will allow them to listen, balance, and weigh your God experience.

Trustworthy people do not pry their way into your life. Instead they wait to be invited by you. They are all about *listening* and *understanding* the thoughts and emotions of others, offering encouragement (inner courage), and a positive, though realistic, view of things. They are very safe confidantes, guarding confidentiality. Once I mentioned to my friend, Bob, that I might send people to him who may need to spill their guts about hard and hurtful things out of their past. Quite abruptly he said, "Well if someone ever comes to me, you will never know about it." Trustworthy people respect personal boundaries. Therefore, they never pressure anyone to share outside of their personal comfort zone. Rather they realize that it is great privilege and honor when someone freely decides to reveal their true inner thoughts and feelings.

Trusted friends give their assessment, critique, and advice very sparingly, usually waiting to be asked for their feedback.

I used to think that a trusted friend should offer lots of good advice. Today I think the opposite, realizing that sometimes my advice is really cloaked criticism. When trusted friends offer critique, they speak it in a positive manner with a respectful tone, and not as a personal attack. They are non-judgmental. Interestingly, we get the English word "critic" from the biblical Greek word for "judge." Trustworthy people view their own assessment of things with hesitation. Hence they know that they do not have God and life all figured out because no one does; therefore, God and life do not operate according to their own personal parameters. Easy answers rarely are offered for complex life situations.

Trusted family and friends are not arrogant. They do not have an over inflated view of themselves. Instead, most of the time (though not all the time), they sincerely and accurately assess their character, both positive and negative. They are able to humbly live in their own humanness and sinfulness. As appropriate, they are open, revealing a true picture of their human nature. Thus pretense or pretending is held to a minimum.

They are not perfect. They know that they are sinners, desperately in need of God's grace, and they are not about hiding this, but are humbly transparent. At times, they may let you down. However when these people wrong and hurt others, they know the importance of honestly taking responsibility, even if it takes time to recognize and admit their wrong doings. Then they acknowledge responsibility, confess their offense, ask for forgiveness, and attempt to make things right. Amazingly, confession and forgiveness give birth to new beginnings. More than once, I have learned this valuable life lesson from humble people.

Trusted and respected people with exceptional character and quality are not common; but, they do exist and they are to be cherished when you find them. Who are the people in your life that most closely resemble these characteristics? Because they are not infallible, you probably will need more than one of them. Who might have this potential if you were to develop a deeper relationship?

Most likely you will need a combination of people who collectively share these exemplary qualities. Maybe you deeply regard a pastor, spiritual director, or even a professional counselor. Perhaps you meet regularly with a Bible study group or a small spiritual formation group. You may significantly trust and respect one or two out of the group. Perhaps join such a group, though certainly this is not needed. Bear in mind for various reasons, not all friends, groups, pastors, spiritual directors, or professional counselors can be quality spiritual friends for you. It is not wrong to come to this conclusion, and invest in finding those friends.

You may trust a small few in this way. Listen to what they see and value in you. On their own, they will offer encouragement. At times you should request their candid impressions and wise counsel as you seek God's call. Take seriously any questions and objections. These people will help to clarify and focus your calling and any guidance received by you.

Sometimes when you believe that you have received God's guidance, you may be mistaken. Your own misplaced motivations or your desire to control people and situations may lead you astray. Therefore, testing your guidance and discerning your call with the help of others is necessary, especially if it has implications for others. Since no guidance should conflict with the Scriptures, other people who know the Scriptures should also confirm this guidance. Your parents, work supervisor, or church leadership (pastors, priests, and other leaders) may function in natural leadership roles over you. Seeking and receiving the affirmation of those in leadership roles is an easy way to test your own impressions.

Unless you are in an unsafe situation, you should seek the perspective of your spouse or your parents (if your parents still financially support you). Because your spouse or parents may be so close to your situation, they may not always offer an impartial viewpoint. Still, God will use them in the process and you should not ignore their impressions. If you are a youth, consider other parental figures from the family of God who might supplement your parents' perceptions with sound insight.

The biblical Greek word for God's Spirit in John 14–16 is "called-alongside one." It can be translated many ways: Encourager, Comforter, Counselor, Advocate, Helper, Intercessor, Strengthener, and Standby. Only God's Spirit is worthy of these exceptional names. Even so, our Lord will call trustworthy and supportive friends with some of these same admirable qualities alongside of you.

"And let us consider how we may spur one another on toward love and good deeds. Let us not give up meeting together, as some are in the habit of doing, but let us encourage one another and all the more as you see the day approaching" (Hebrews 10:24–25, NIV).

Called to the Great Reversal

The writer of Ecclesiastes tells us that God has placed eternity in our hearts (Ecclesiastes 3:11). We not only long for eternity out in the future, but we are called and wired to make a mark or leave a legacy that will last unto eternity. A passionate piece of God's eternal vision is wired within you.

An endless sea of needs compete for your concern, compassion, and time. The world is just plain broken. Problems abound everywhere around us. Families are fractured by grief, broken relationships, distrust, lying, and busyness. Much needs fixing in the workplace as well. How about the inability to work together, greed, gossip, or negativity? Neighborhoods struggle with inadequate housing, litter, and crime. What are the challenges of your community and world? Poverty, war, disease, and the destruction of creation are ever present somewhere on the planet. A list of problems, struggles, and brokenness would quickly lengthen. In fact, the real list is infinitely long. Evil, death, and sin are manifest in all shapes and sizes. You may be called to solve one or more of these burdensome problems.

Conversely and ideally speaking, if you were to imagine a perfect world, what would this look like to you? Peace and prosperity, happiness and hope, trust and truth, joy and justice might be apt descriptors. In short, you could say the absence of all those problems. This perfect picture might be entitled goodness or blessedness, or you also might label this idyllic existence as heaven. Heaven is God's divine imagination made into reality. Of course, God's imagination far surpasses our own pitiful imaginations.

Though you may not realize it, how you imagine or envision heaven will in no small way influence your hopes and expectations of what God can do for you and through you right now.

When I used to think about heaven, I was a bit baffled. I could not imagine what I would do. I wondered if I would be bored. Then, I heard a powerful sermon, describing a vision of heaven. It was a glimpse of God's extraordinary heavenly vision. Because this message significantly impacted my own life, I later preached nearly the same sermon. Not many days later, a woman shared with me how my proclamation increased her own vision for attacking poverty and hunger. Days and even weeks later, others expressed deep desires and compassionate concerns for our world, and how they each personally wanted to make a difference. Your own vision of heaven will enable you to see more clearly your passions and burdens for our world. This connection between your vision of heaven and your own passions and burdens may seem puzzling to you.

Allow me to recreate a bit of the sermon that so powerfully transformed my own vision. Though most definitely not all of these details are accurate, the basic message is grounded in Scripture. As you reflect upon this heavenly vision, invite God to ignite and expand your own imagination and vision.

God's Heavenly Vision

Heaven is the very best of the best. Streets will be paved in gold and all things will be made of the finest things. The extraordinary beauty of God will be all around: the greatest mountains, the most extraordinary gardens, the bluest clearest rivers and lakes, and the forests will be filled with exquisite fall color. God's light will shine continually.

Heaven is a place of the greatest intellect and creativity. In heaven, each of us will be able to learn from all the very best and greatest masters of all time in all their variety and creativity: the greatest musicians, the greatest crafts people and artists, the greatest thinkers, writers, scholars and inventors, and the greatest athletes. If you are a person with no physical ability in this life and you have a hidden desire to be a gymnast, this will be possible in heaven.

Heaven will have the very best party and the most wonderful celebration ever. You will have the most fun. Whatever is fun to you, the depth of *fun* in heaven will be better.

Heaven is where great reversals become reality. A whole new creation is established (Revelation 21:1–7). Heaven will be everything good and right. Boredom will be reversed and replaced by real fulfillment, purpose, and meaning. Love will replace hate. The great *yes* of God will replace critique. Laughter will replace tears. Happiness will replace sadness. Joy will replace mourning. Peaceful relationships characterized by true, loyal, and authentic friendship will replace hurtfulness, falsehood, pretense, enmity, conflict, and war. Health, wholeness, equality, and justice will replace brokenness, sickness, racism, and poverty. Struggle, problems, sin, death, and evil will be absent. Instead, God's goodness will be everlasting and present in everything. Yes! Heaven is a place of great reversals.

Heaven is where the greatest, most fulfilling and uninterrupted friendship with God is possible. You will know your Lord's profound love for you in a way that you could never have imagined. As a result, God's values and character will be honored and desired by all. The scriptures tell us that "No eye has seen, no ear has heard, no mind has conceived what God has prepared for those who love him" (1 Corinthians 2:9, NIV). Though what I have described might sound good to you, it is not the real heavenly vision. Heaven will be much better.[1]

Though you may anticipate and long for heaven in the future, God also desires for heaven to become a reality on earth. Heaven represents God's imagination, vision, and desires for this world. Heaven captures our Lord's ingenious and masterful plan for our existence. The kingdom of heaven is not merely a place to accommodate eternal life beyond death; rather, it is wherever God is ruling and reigning right here and right now.

Already the kingdom of heaven or the rule and reign

of God has permanently come to earth in a person named Jesus. At the very start of his ministry, Jesus began to proclaim this good news by saying, "Repent, for the kingdom of heaven has come near" (Matthew 4:17, NRSV). Then, he began to demonstrate the great reversal by forgiving people's failures and wrongs, casting out evil, healing, and bringing wholeness where there was brokenness, calling people to a relationship with himself, and teaching them heavenly values and character. He announced the advent of his rule and reign saying, "Blessed are the poor in spirit, for theirs is the kingdom of heaven. Blessed are those who mourn, for they will be comforted. Blessed are ... " (Matthew 5:3–5, NIV). With an extraordinary use of heavenly power, Jesus has brought the rule and reign of God from heaven to earth with his presence and love. Jesus was not just alive two thousand years ago, but he is alive today. The kingdom of heaven did not die on a cross or get buried in a tomb, but it is alive and well today wherever God is ruling and reigning. Impossible problems can be turned into passionate possibilities. Jesus has launched a great reversal.

To consider heaven is to contemplate what God desires for your life right here and right now. This is why Jesus taught you to pray, "Your kingdom come, your will be done on earth as it is in heaven." God's heavenly rule and reign is available to you. A new creation is underway. Whatever you need, whatever your lot in life, whatever evil there is, whatever is hard or difficult or not good for you, Jesus has come from heaven to earth for you. The kingdom of heaven is available to you, but not just you—others too. A great reversal has begun.

Still now, Jesus continues to establish his heavenly vision

as a reality on earth through people like you and me. God has custom designed and empowered ordinary people like you to continue this mission and to make God's heavenly vision for this world into a reality. Wherever the rule and reign of God can be found, the extraordinary is happening.

So how does God's heavenly vision motivate you? Your passions and burdens are a piece of God's eternal vision. Perhaps you will be a problem breaker in contrast to a problem-maker or a problem-evaluator. Problem-evaluators most often are problem-makers, astutely critiquing, judging, and pointing out problems while doing little to positively address them. What problem would you like to solve? What burdens bother you? More beauty, more creativity, more truth, more justice, more grace, and more mercy—do you think that our world needs more of these? Well, maybe you will be a goodness-maker or a heaven-maker. What are your passions and dreams for positive possibilities? Then again, maybe you will create and prepare still more problem-breakers and goodness-makers. In other words, you might be an equipper. Could be that you will launch still more equippers. In fact, if you are an equipper, you likely possess one of the "equipping" spiritual gifts—teachers, shepherds, prophets, evangelists, or apostles. Problem breaker, goodness maker, or equipper—most likely your passions and burdens will be a bit of all three.

What would it look like if God were ruling and reigning in every person and every place on this earth? How will you make God's heavenly vision into a reality in your work, family, church, neighborhood, community, and world? God longs to give you heavenly horizons and hopes.

Living with Vision and Passion

God custom designs and calls ordinary everyday people like you to do the extraordinary. Sometimes extraordinary people are labeled "saints." You too are called to be a saint, someone who has been set apart and claimed to establish God's extraordinary rule and reign on earth. You were set apart through God's heavenly words and water. You were filled with God's heavenly Spirit, his heavenly power, and his heavenly gifts. The riches of God's heavenly kingdom were made available to you. Even if you are called to something that appears small, to God it is great and glorious.

With their words and actions, passionate people of God—past and present—have demonstrated the availability of God's heavenly rule and reign. William Wilberforce, a British politician tirelessly battled the slave trade in Britain until it was miraculously abolished. Year after year, Mother Teresa offered hope to the broken and poor of India. Frank Laubach championed adult literacy. Through the Bible, TV, books, and Internet, ordinary people like these can motivate you with their stories and testimonials. They are remarkable mentors and examples. They are kingdom people who lived according to God's call and under God's rule and reign. Like me, some of your personal friends may inspire you. You can celebrate and applaud each of their calls. They can teach you through their experiences, failures, fears, joys, and successes.

When you hear moving stories, you might begin to compare yourself to these impressive people. You might wonder or even *fear* that God may call you to some of the same things. This is not the purpose of hearing their stories. Rather be enthused that God desires to uniquely call and use you.

By now, you know that God has given me a personal vision and passion to ignite and equip others to seek their heavenly calling. Instead of living according to others' expectations or just going with the flow, I can imagine a motivated multitude making our Lord's heavenly vision into reality. Often God endows me with a spiritual gift of faith, causing me to really believe that it's going to happen—although not exactly how I expect. God supernaturally guides and moves me in this pursuit. I relentlessly teach, preach, write, and lead, taking steps through various doors and opportunities along the way. Frequently, God calls other people to walk and work alongside me. Together we can envision it—a bit of heaven happening on earth.

Burdens are being battled. A great reversal is underway. Heavenly passions and purposes have been planted in people. Ordinary people are becoming extraordinary. People are "pressing on toward the goal of the heavenly call of God in Christ Jesus" (Philippians 3:14). Your call is a "heavenly call"—part of God's "heavenly" vision for this world.

"'No eye has seen, no ear has heard, no mind has conceived what God has prepared for those who love him'—but God has revealed it to us by his Spirit" (1 Corinthians 2:9–10a, NIV).

Called to Take Steps and Walk

So how is the adventure? Where are you now? Looking back, how far have you come? Are you at a fork along the way? Are you wondering where to head next?

Sit for a bit. Rest. Pause. Here is a promise penned for you. "The Lord will fulfill his purpose for me; your love, O LORD, endures forever—do not abandon the works of your hands" (Psalm 138:8, NIV).

What might be around the next bend? God is beckoning you. Follow. Keep pressing on. Important steps are ahead!

Some are mini steps. Some are small steps. Custom design your steps. First take one step and then another. One step will lead you to the next, keep on walking!

Mini Steps

Describe the scenery: Where are you? What is happening right now? Jim unexpectedly lost his wife. Disarmed, life seemed to pause for an awfully long time. Have you paused? Are you in transition? Do you feel any of these normal emotions? Hopeful? Optimistic? Encouraged? Restless? Anxious? Overwhelmed? Worried? Discontent? Unsettled? Discouraged? Afraid? Hurting? Grieving? Confused? Empty? Guilty? Lost? Make an attempt to specifically describe your feelings. You may uncover a clue, leading to the next step. Picture and know that God is with you (Matthew 28:20). God cares for you (1 Peter 5:7). God knows your feelings and what you need right now (Hebrews 4:12–16).

Have patience and allow God to put the puzzle together: You have a BIG God. Do what makes sense today. Right now this is what God is calling you to do. Then wait for God to show you what to do tomorrow and the next day. Putting the pieces together will not happen overnight or even in a few days, but it likely will take some time. Have a long-term view. Try to avoid false starts. Do not be impulsive or reactive. Do not jump into something. Do not get ahead of yourself. Often God's timing is not our timing.

Reconsider those two key questions—even the third question: "Who am I?" "What am I to do?" "How and where do I find the answers?" Which is a mystery for you? That "Who am I?" question once was baffling for me. Begin with the one that is most puzzling to you.

Find your fans: Who will encourage and support you? Begin to identify friends and family members that you trust and respect. Who are your cheerleaders? Who do you deeply respect for their insight and wisdom, especially spiritual insight and wisdom? To whom could you bare your soul, sharing your true thoughts and feelings? Who does or might pray consistently for you if asked? Who encourages you to grow as a person in a non-threatening, affirming, and even healing way? Who do you feel comfortable asking for their feedback and advice?

Track your thoughts: In no particular order and at no pre-planned time, significant thoughts will come to you. God's Spirit within you will speak to you using your thoughts. Record and collect important insights.

Minimize your mental hurdles: What prevents you from running the race? Remember those hurdles in the beginning? Which hurdles are hindering you? How can you minimize or neutralize these hurdles? Ask God to give you wisdom (James 1:5). Request God to remove them.

Inventory your fears: What concerns do you have? What do you most fear? Remember God is not the author of fear. Often our Lord has said, "Do not be afraid." Exposing and confronting your fears can take away their paralyzing effect. Contemplate your Lord's grace and love for you (John 14:27, Joshua 1:9, Psalm 27:13–14). God is for you, not against you (Romans 8:31).

Search for scripture to be your ally: When I was a teenager, my Bible study leader understood that God's Word was living, active, and powerful. Repeatedly she quoted words like, "So shall my word be that goes out from my mouth; it shall not return to me empty, but it shall accomplish that which I purpose" (Isaiah 55:11, NRSV). God's Word will guide and transform you. Attack your fears, insecurities, and other challenging emotions with God's Word. Though they may not disappear, hope, peace, and wisdom may invade in the midst of these feelings. Collect scripture and other wisdom that causes you to be hopeful, inspired, encouraged, and optimistic. Listen to music that offers the same type of inspiration. Use a concordance, promise book, or ask a pastor or priest to help you. From my own personal search for meaningful scripture, I compiled a list entitled *Diminishing Difficulties with God's Powerful Promises*–found in Appendix B.

Consider the state of your faith: Present your state of the union address to a friend. What has God already done in your life? When have you most experienced our Lord's presence? Be encouraged! Where do you have hang-ups? Maybe you feel forsaken or you feel like you have been dealt a horrible lot in life. Maybe someone has deeply hurt you. Maybe you are angry with God about something. Maybe you know religious people that you really do not like. You do not need to be like them. Maybe you have regrets. Maybe you feel trapped by something. Maybe your experience of church has been all about running an institution—prodding you to do certain things or getting your money or building a building. Maybe you do not like or believe part of the Bible for one reason or another. Maybe you do not like certain religious words. God can handle all of your hang-ups. Talk to God about them. If needed, shout! Be honest. Be angry. Cry or even weep. Jesus used a psalm to cry out, "My God, my god, why have you forsaken me?" (Psalm 22:1, NRSV). The Psalms show us that these kinds of prayers are permissible with God.

Find a church and worship regularly: If you try a church and it is not the right one for you, try another until you find one that fits you. Churches come in all shapes and sizes, but hopefully all are centered in the Gospel of Jesus. Look for a church where you experience, encounter, and worship the living Jesus who is for you and not against you (Romans 8:31). Look for a church where you feel comfortable and you can be yourself. Look for a church where you can grow in knowing Jesus. Look for a group of people where you come away knowing that your wrongs, failures, and sins are forgiven—past, present, and future. Look for a church gathering where you hear good news from God's Word. Look for a church where you are fed and nourished by bread and wine. Look for a church gathering where you come away feeling helped, encouraged and inspired. Remember a church is not an institution, but rather a group of imperfect people who want to know Jesus just like you and me. Because this is true, not all of these characteristics will be present all the time. Remember Christianity and the church is about having the greatest relationship with Jesus made possible by his death and resurrection. Once you find the right church for you, make a personal commitment to stay there and to gather and worship weekly with the other believers.

Free up five minutes in your day in order to spend intentional time with your Lord: Consider where you spend your time on something unimportant or insignificant or where you waste a few minutes in your day. What can wait till later? When are you the least distracted by people, telephones, and your list of things to do? Morning? Evening? Another time? Possibly look for the first available time when other things can wait till later? What will you do with these five minutes? Read a verse or two from scripture? Do what works best for you. Nearly everyday, I quote specific Scripture passages to myself that are inspirational to me. Here is an idea or two. Rest in our Lord's love and allow it to cover you. Pray. Listen for God's gentle whisper. Use a devotional. Repeat the Jesus prayer, "Lord Jesus Christ, Son of God, have mercy on me a sinner." There is no one right way to spend your five minutes.

Continually invite the Holy Spirit to fill you: Right now all by yourself, you can ask the Holy Spirit to fill you. Tomorrow and the next day, you can pray this same request again. The Holy Spirit will give you life, guide you, and empower you. Ask someone to lay their hands upon you, praying that the Spirit would fill and empower all that you think, say, or do. Come Holy Spirit! If you have never been baptized, find out more from a pastor or priest.

Focus on Jesus. Carry on a conversation with your Lord: Jesus already knows what is going on with you, and He understands all of it. Therefore, talk to him about anything and everything (Philippians 4:6–7). Offer your thoughts and emotions to him. As much as possible through your day, picture Jesus with you, praying for you. He is even praying for you right now (Hebrews 7:25).

Compose a personal letter to God: Begin by offering thanks. Detail your hopes, dreams, and deepest desires for life. Solicit your Lord's help where you trip and fall. Ask God for the character qualities that you most need. Invite your Lord to be involved in all of your life. Ask God to take away your fears. Thank God for what he has already done in your life, and all the many gifts that you have received. Consider praying this letter every day. Many years ago I wrote my own personal letter and since then, I have prayed it nearly every day.

Sample ideas: Brainstorm ideas all by yourself and also with others. Create a big list of problems. As food for thought, do specific Internet searches. For example, solicit various types of employment opportunities. Try on your ideas. Do they fit you? Which is uncomfortable? As I attempted to find the right college major for me, I tried on various fields of study. Though I rarely could find one that felt right for me, still the experience was insightful. As you become more focused, try a small task to confirm whether your ideas fit you. Take a short-term assignment. Does this sampling energize you? Consider why or why not.

Keep a journal: Jot down your thoughts, ideas, fears, inspirations, revelations, and impressions whenever it works for you—even if very sporadically. Do not make this into a hard exercise. Use your journal as a tool to take action.

Locate the source of your energy: What rises to the surface? What first floats into your mind? Which section of this book is front and center for you? Which created excitement within you? Take it in again slowly and reflectively this time, inviting God to invade your thoughts. Share your impressions with one of your trustworthy friends.

Have realistic expectations: Along the way, you will have false starts and failures. Throughout your life, you will discover hurdles, issues, frustrations, and other detours that you will need to overcome and leave behind. For some of these distractions, you will need perseverance to get beyond them. Hurtful and hard things may require help. It will be well worth it on the other side. You may have discovered some obstacles and barriers already. Do not get sidetracked by these. Jesus will very carefully and gently provide for you over and over again, giving you needed wisdom and help (Hebrews 12:1–2).

Small Steps

Free up an hour or two to take a small step: How could you rearrange your time? Spend less time on the trivial in order to create time for more significant matters.

Seek to know, follow, and uniquely serve Jesus by pursuing spiritual growth: Invite Jesus to rule and reign in your life. Survey and explore various time-tested spiritual practices or disciplines that intentionally place you in your Lord's presence to receive his grace. Ask for suggestions from a pastor, priest, spiritual director, or other faithful person. Try some of the practices throughout this volume. Focus on those that seem right for this season of your life.

Study your history—recognize how far you have come in your life: Review your life's journey. Recognize your accomplishments. Identify your strengths and weaknesses. Ponder your aspirations and hopes. Acknowledge your regrets. Reflect upon the key points. Summarize important insights. Look carefully for any God sightings! What is your legacy thus far?

Contemplate your custom design: Review and record your unique attributes and spiritual gifts. Allow some time to pass—maybe a couple of weeks. Then reflect upon your God-given uniqueness again. Repeat your review, collecting and recording any new revelations. Solicit the observations of your friends and family. Ask them to describe your custom design—your talents, skills, abilities, personality, passions, and spiritual gifts. What is missing? God will continue to reveal new insights to you.

Begin identifying your spiritual gifts: Reflect upon the descriptions of each spiritual gift. Try an inventory or one of the other ways to identify your spiritual gifts. Refer to

Diagram B in the spiritual gifts chapter. Remember that you are endowed with competencies that will motivate you.

Experiment with your spiritual gifts: Seek small opportunities that match your uniqueness. Wait for the right situation to present itself. Try new things that are attractive to you. Volunteer for a short period of time. If you are not enjoying one of your present activities, consider why. If needed, stop doing it.

List roles where God has placed you right now: Record your roles at work—engineer, doctor, supervisor, student, friend, or co-worker—to name a few examples. Note your roles in your family—father, sister, son, or wife. List your roles at your church gathering—leader, teacher, hospitality greeter, usher, choir member, coordinator, or children's worker. Name your roles in your neighborhood, community, and world—neighbor, friend, school board, Girl Scout leader, volunteer, missionary, community leader, or politician. What is fulfilling or not fulfilling? In order for Tammy to balance being a stay-at-home mom, her daughters' Girl Scout leader and a hospice volunteer, she had to give up serving on a couple of committees.

Intentionally and periodically reflect upon your heartfelt desires: Ask God's Spirit to inspire you, using your thoughts, God's Word, and other people. Consider your heartfelt desires for all of these roles and arenas: your relationship with Jesus, your relationship with your spouse, your marriage, your children and parenting, your extended family, your friends, your work or vocation—present and future, management of your household, your spiritual gifts, your uniqueness, your involvement in your neighborhood, community and world, your church, your desires for intellect and learning, your leisure time hobbies and fun, your personal growth, your character desires, your emotional and physical wellness, your finances and material goods, and even your retirement. "Delight yourself in the Lord, and he will give you the desires of your heart" (Psalm 37:4, NIV).

Listen to God's Word and gentle whisper: God's Spirit will inspire and guide you, giving you specific, practical, and personal wisdom. Try an idea or two from the inspiration chapter. Talk to a pastor, priest, spiritual director, or someone else who understands these spiritual disciplines.

Seek reliable counsel: Pick a couple of people that you trust and respect. What would you most like to discuss? Make a mental outline. Set up some time to talk. Share your thoughts and impressions while inviting perspective, feedback, and impressions. Over the years, the insightful advice that I have received from others has amazed me.

Join a group: You can always quit. You should never feel compelled to stay in any group. Gather with a group where either your faith or friendships can grow. There is no guarantee that this will happen. Try a focus group with people who share a common calling. Start a group by hand picking and inviting others to come together with you.

Gain inspiration from extraordinary people: Study great people in the Bible and throughout history. Why were they exemplary? Ponder their lives and imitate their ways. Listen to their testimonials or read their biographies. Learn about someone who shares similar interests with you. William and Catherine Booth attacked homelessness in London.

Create a personal mission statement(s): Similar to a corporation or church, compose a personal mission statement. A personal mission statement can more sharply focus your life.

Perhaps write several mission statements for various facets of your life–family or work. Attempt to capture life-defining goals with a few words.

Custom design a pattern of life: Created by you, a pattern of life is a blueprint or plan for your life. Your unique pattern will reflect your call, integrating together various insights, needed steps, and helpful practices with your circumstances and lifestyle. It will intentionally assist you in developing a deep and profound friendship with Jesus. Later, you will have an opportunity to custom design your own pattern.

Build your confidence: Daily watch for how our Lord encourages you—perhaps using God's Word or one of your friends. Consider how your life could be enhanced if you were to acquire more experience, training, skills, and knowledge. Where do you lack confidence? What are the obstacles that prevent you from moving ahead? Confronting obstacles is up next.

Be an apprentice or intern: Assist and shadow someone who has expertise or experience that you respect. Try on their role. Does this role fit you? What would you alter and change? When young, Candy was so fascinated by watching a speech therapist that now for over thirty years, she has pursued the same fulfilling path.

Press on to know Jesus: If you are overwhelmed or caught in complexity, take the wise advice of my friend: "Don't worry so much about these things. Don't even think about them. Instead, make it your number one goal in life to know Jesus and then all else will fall into place." This goal will be sufficient. Remember Jesus is all about having a relationship with you. God has created you. God is calling you, and God is quite capable of getting you to the place that is best and custom designed for you. Be hopeful! Down the road, you will wake up one morning and suddenly realize that our Lord has very carefully put all the pieces together for you. Then quite spontaneously, you will offer praise and thanksgiving to your Lord and Savior Jesus for graciously working in your life.

Walk!

Prayerfully choose a direction by taking a couple of steps. Begin to walk. Pause and adjust your course. When the time is right for you—today, tomorrow, or next month—take additional steps. Remember God is walking faithfully and steadfastly with you!

"Now to him who is able to do far more abundantly beyond all that we ask or think, according to the power that works within us, to him be the glory in the church [called-out-ones] and in Christ Jesus to all generations forever and ever. Amen. Therefore I, the prisoner of the Lord, implore [earnestly call] you to *walk* in a manner worthy of the calling with which you have been called" (Ephesians 3:20–4:1, NASB) (author's own translation in brackets).

"The one who calls you is faithful, and he will do this" (1 Thessalonians 5:24, NRSV).

Called to a Wise Economy of Life

How is the economy of your life? Trapped, frustrated, restless—do these characterize you? Freedom and versatility—sounds appealing but too good to be true? All of these may be clues that you are not living in the fullness of how God has custom designed and called you. Rearranging the pieces and certainly adding something new may seem like an unattainable and impossible luxury to you. You are called to be a wise economist.

Many years ago, I lived and traveled with six other young adults in West Africa. From city to town to small village, we trekked from place to place for many months. At times, the poverty felt shocking. Near the end of our stint, our group stayed in a simple guestroom with cement floors and walls—freshly painted white. All of us had a comfortable bed. We shared a clean and simple bathroom. Compared to previous nights, this guesthouse was like a palace. We had each other. We had food. We each had a few changes of clothes. We had Jesus in our lives. We knew how to find purpose in life. We knew how to make up our own fun. One day as I darted into the room, God gently interrupted my thoughts: "You have everything you need right here." In a moment of time, many words took on new meaning... need, want, contentment, wealth.

Minute by minute and day-by-day, your life is unfolding while spending choices compete for your time, money, and resources. Either your spending choices will detour you from your call, or your call can determine and direct your spending choices. Practicing the principles of God's economy will lead to wise spending by you.

Gift and Provision vs. Ownership

God is the giver and provider of everything good! This most fundamental of facts will keep your life in proper perspective, influencing all of your choices and decisions.

All was well for some friends, or at least so it seemed. Then through a series of unusual circumstances out of their control, the provider of the family suddenly became unemployed, losing both excellent pay and a high position. In the confusion of this loss, the couple knelt and cried out to God for help. They had children and significant bills. Very quickly, they became aware that God needed to be their provider. Intentionally recognizing God as their provider suddenly made sense like never before. Not too long later, they found a dollar bill in their garage. For them, this bill was a sign.

God was their provider. They decided to give the money to God, placing it in the offering plate at their church.

What goods of life has God given to you? Your list probably would include all of these goods: salvation, identity, calling, purpose for living, relationships (family and friends), time (the hours, days, and years that God gives you), work, spiritual gifts, talents, skills, abilities, material resources, name, beauty, pleasure, food, clothing, shelter, water, and the earth. Freely and graciously, you were given a "trust" to manage, spend, and multiply. Really you could call it abundance of life. Jesus said, "The thief comes only to steal and kill and destroy. I came that they may have life, and have it abundantly" (John 10:10, NRSV).

Sometimes we all have trouble with the truth. Do you ever tell yourself any of these subtle lies? I am the maker and creator of my goods. I am the owner of my goods. I am the producer of all my goods. I am the creator of my ability to produce. I obtained my job. I am the creator of my time. In reality though, your job, your time, and even your ability to accomplish, are all gifts (Deuteronomy 8:1–18).

Principle No. 1: God is your Provider! Therefore, God can take good care of you, freeing you from needless worry and stress (Matthew 6:25–34).

Wise Management vs. Wasteful Spending

From the biblical Greek word for stewardship, we get our word economy. Stewardship is about having a wise economy of life. You are called to be a wise steward. Steward in the biblical Greek literally means household manager. Stewardship is the wise management of your life. It is about building your house or building your life. Stewardship is not a program or effort at church which for many can create an, "Ugh." Thankfully, stewardship is a personal lifestyle. Stewardship is the wise management of all the goods given and entrusted to you.

Using nearly all of my part-time wages, I once hired some cleaning help. I figured that I would rather work a bit filling people's lives with faith than clean my house. Time and money have a very important relationship in this economy of your life. Like me, you can use your time to make money, or you can use your money to free up your time. You can also spend less time making money and live on less. In turn, you can use the extra time for another purpose. You can also decide to have less stuff. Then you will spend less time maintaining all of your stuff, and more time *living more with less*. That's appealing to me. *Living More with Less* by Doris Janzen Longacre offers helpful and practical tips.

Managing your God-given allotment of goods is no more than a series of choices. These choices will reflect your priorities. Some choices and priorities will result in joy and fulfillment while others will lead to frustration, stress, and restlessness. God desires that your choices would be characterized by goodness, wholeness, completeness, order, balance, grace, and whole relationships with God, others, creation and yourself (Genesis 1–2). In other words, wise stewardship results in abundant, healthy, and fruitful living.

Jesus taught about three stewards and how they each spent, managed, and multiplied their goods of life (not just money). Their lord or master entrusted each of them with an allotment of his property. Of course, our Lord's property is everything in existence. Two of the stewards multiplied their goods of life, and the master gave them more. One steward did nothing with his goods of life because he falsely feared that his lord was harsh and would take away his goods. Of course, the master did not take away the goods of the other two. So, how well did the third steward really know his master?

What kind of steward are you? How will you spend your gifts of life? What choices will you make? What priorities will govern these choices? What kind of accounting will you give when our Lord returns? (Matthew 25:14–30).

Principle No. 2: God has called you to be a prudent steward, wisely managing your allotment of life's goods.

Needs vs. Wants

Needs are essential. Without them, you would not be fully living. Distinguish between need and want. Wise living will result.

Many times, I have prayed: "Lord, show me a way to satisfy my want." When my kids were young, I really wanted a bit more time for myself. Childcare was not affordable for us. God gave me an idea. My friends and I began to exchange childcare. For eight years, we traded with three other families. Joel and I even had a weekly date night that we rarely missed. All the kids became the best of friends. There even was an added bonus. All the adults became good friends as well.

While living in Africa, I found out that I could get along quite well without all kinds of stuff. Yes! I do have all kinds of stuff. However, I know that if needed, I can pass by all kinds of things and say no to all kinds of desires. Though

Jesus warned about the perils of wealth, both the poor and rich were his disciples. He cared for both. Many people of wealth even provided for Jesus' needs. To Jesus, the rich are those who have more than they need. According to Jesus, I am rich. Yes! I am very rich! Unfortunately in my culture, the rich are defined as those who have more than "me."

Principle No. 3: God is the source of all *life* and the owner of all your *goods*. God will provide for your needs, and sometimes fulfill even your wants (Psalm 23).

Overextension vs. Simplicity

Subtle falsehood can be a real problem in your economy of life. Do you ever tell yourself any of these lies? "I have to have it now...I have to do it now...I will never get it for this price again...I need it." Almost always, "I need a new dress," should be "I want a new dress," since beautiful dresses already line your closet.

Often overextension is self-inflicted. It is caused by an inability to wait or say no. Overextension of your money creates unwise debt. Carrying a large balance beyond the grace period on your credit card easily leaves a burden of not only debt, but also stress and anxiety. In turn, high payments eliminate your spending choices, trading your freedom for bondage. Overextension of your time multiplies stress and anxiety while destroying the ability to relax, have fun, be present to other people, and focus on important priorities.

Simplicity is the opposite of overextension. Simplicity is not ridding yourself of all possessions and never enjoying life.

In her best-selling book, *The Not So Big House,* architect Sarah

Susanka advocates designing a home that maximizes space and beauty, rather than building a big structure. Sounds logical, yet common sense and practicality are too easily left behind.

True simplicity is built upon the simple fact that only Jesus can bring contentment—whether you have a lot or a little. In turn, simplicity is promoted and sustained by moderation, self-discipline, and common sense. With moderation, still you can partake and enjoy, though perhaps less often or in a less expensive manner. Since the purpose of a car is to get you from point A to point B, perhaps you could get along quite well with a little less expensive car. Self-discipline permits you to say yes and no at the proper times (Philippians 4:6–14, 1 Timothy 6:6–10). Mary Poppins of Disney fame wisely proclaimed: "Enough is as good as a feast."

Principle No. 4: True simplicity will save you from the slavery of overextension.

Being Driven vs. God's Gift of the Sabbath

More than ever, we need the Sabbath day. We need to cease, rest, enjoy, receive, and be nourished by God's Word and grace. The Sabbath rest can provide needed time for God, spouse, children, and friends.

When I was young, every week our family practiced the Sabbath rest. Together we would worship, eat a meal, and perhaps go for an afternoon ride. Sometimes friends would share the day with us. Of course, it was easier when places of business were closed and most people did not work. My parents and elders still model the Sabbath rest.

The Sabbath rest is a gift from God. The Sabbath is a day set aside to cease from the activities of your week and in turn, embrace activities and values that bring refreshment and restoration. Creating a rhythm of ceasing and embracing will keep your life in proper perspective. The Sabbath will protect you from anxiety and overextension. It is not a demanding law ordering you to do nothing or requiring you to worship. The Sabbath rest is a way of living.

The Hebrew word for Sabbath is translated "cease." Instead of working, paying your bills, and washing your clothes, embrace and celebrate God's values and ways. Worship. Listen to God's Word and gentle whisper. Be with family and friends. Experience grace. Embrace wholeness. Surround yourself with beauty. Love. Laugh. Celebrate. Have fun. The Sabbath way of living is not a "have to do it," but rather another "get to do it" practice. God longs to give spiritual, emotional, intellectual, and physical rest. The Sabbath rest will both sustain you through the week as you remember it, and give you hope as you anticipate and await its coming. The Sabbath rest was so important to God that it is one of the Ten Commandments— the "ten best ways to live."

Principle No. 5: The Sabbath way of living will rescue you from being driven, providing time for relaxation and recreating what is missing in your life.

Investing in the Kingdom vs. Idolatry, Greed, Anxiety, and Covetousness

Many times, possessions and the love of money can control and possess us rather than the other way around. We can have so much stuff that all our time is "possessed" and consumed by acquiring, managing, and maintaining all of it (Luke 12:15–21). Being possessed by possessions far too easily creates frivolous choices, unwise living, and finally bondage.

During the Lenten preparation season, my husband and I once visited a priest to confess our sins. Though we owned much less back then, I still confessed that too often I worried about money and material things. After the priest offered forgiveness, he suggested that I give away something of value to work against my greed and covetousness. He knew a secret that surprised me.

Idolatry is having false gods. A false god is not only a golden statue. Rather it is anything that you fear, love, and trust more than the one true God who gives and provides everything. Your priorities and spending choices indicate the "first" loves of your life. They indicate where you place your trust and where you look in time of need.

If you really know who owns and provides the goods, then possessing them is unnecessary because they are not yours. Instead, you can give them away. Investing in God's work increases joy and decreases the grip of greed, anxiety, and idolatry. When grace—the great, big everything given by God—moves your heart, cheerful and generous giving becomes a natural spontaneous desire. When our living Lord's grace transformed my parents' lives, overnight they shifted from giving very little to offering a tithe of their resources to God.

The tithe is giving back to God the first and best ten percent of your provision, and then trusting God to provide for you with the rest. The tithe is a gift from God to protect you from falsely thinking that you have made, earned, or own your provision. If duty and obligation do not motivate tithing, then you will constantly be reminded that God is your provider. Occasionally, I have wondered whether I should continue tithing. Always the question runs through my mind, *Is God really my provider?* I must come to grips with my answer.

The tithe is not any kind of requirement that everyone must follow. Rather, beginning in Old Testament times and continuing today, God's people have found that tithing keeps money in proper perspective. If you truly believe that God is your provider, then giving your first ten percent will not be difficult. Neither will it be hard to believe that God can adequately provide for your needs—in ways perhaps unforeseen to you. In fact, our Lord through the prophet Malachi challenged the people and you to "test God" by giving the tithe, and then see if God would not pour out many blessings (Malachi 3:8–12).

Remember those friends who abruptly lost the job and later found the dollar bill in their garage? Prior to this painful loss, they had absolutely no desire to tithe. However when they cried out to God for provision, they suddenly decided to begin tithing and placed the dollar in the offering plate as a symbol of their decision.

Offerings of any amount always have represented sacrificing oneself to God. During our weekly offering in my tradition, we pray these truthful and meaningful words:

> *We offer with joy and thanksgiving what you have first given us—our selves, our time, and our possessions, signs of your gracious love. Receive them for the sake of him who offered himself for us, Jesus Christ our Lord. AMEN.*[1]

Principle No. 6: Investing in God's work will release you from the grip of possessions, greed, anxiety, and even idolatry.

Sharing vs. Possessing

When God's people mutually share their common faith in Jesus with one another, his Spirit also will motivate them to share their other goods of life in common. One of my heartfelt desires for home and family is to share with other families.

While composing this manuscript, I stayed for many days at my friends' ranch—their getaway place. As I wrote, I was alone in the quiet. I couldn't imagine completing this endeavor at home, trying to balance writing with managing a home, spending time with my family, and dealing with innumerable distractions.

By sharing their ranch with me, my friends actually participated in the book's publishing. In other words, the fruit of my efforts also belongs to them. In a sense, they have said, "What is ours is also yours." I do not own a bit of their ranch, but because of their sharing, I am richer in ways beyond using their ranch. Over the years, we have shared our lives and faith with each other, and now even their ranch. I appreciate the ranch, and this alone makes me richer. In reality though, the friendship makes me wealthier yet.

The vastness of our Lord's grace motivates me to say to my family, friends, and others that I care about, "What is mine is available to you." We can share not only our tangible possessions, but also our non-tangibles, such as our time, joys, and struggles. When people would build barns for one another, they not only completed a needed task, but they enjoyed a rich social time together. Sharing between those who "have" and those who "have not" creates a fair and just distribution of the tangible and non-tangible goods of life.

If you and I were more conscious of the power of sharing, we probably could have fewer possessions. We could even co-own much more. We could give away more. We could eliminate need. We could spend less time working—allowing our time to be free for other purposes.

Principle No. 7: Sharing can create greater freedom and versatility with your choices and even enrich the lives of others.

Wearing a "Coat of Many Colors"

"Coat of Many Colors" is an autobiographical song and children's book written by Dolly Parton. Recalling her humble beginnings, Parton relays how her mother lovingly stitched a beautiful coat:

> *My coat of many colors that my mama made for me, made only from rags. But I wore it so proudly and though we had no money I was rich as I could be, in my coat of many colors my mama made for me.*

While sewing, her mother told the Old Testament story of Joseph and his coat of many colors. With holes in her shoes and patches on her pants, she wore the coat to school. As others poked fun, Parton shares her reaction:

> *And I told them all the story mama told me as she sewed, and how my coat of many colors was worth more than all their*

gold. But they didn't understand it and I tried to make
them see that one is only poor if they choose to be
> *And though we had no money I was rich as I could*
be in my coat of many colors that mama made for me.[2]

The coat of many colors symbolizes so many of God's values and principles for a wise economy of life. God has clothed you with a coat of many colors. Put it on and wear it well.

"Be careful then how you live, not as unwise people but as wise, making the most of the time, because the days are evil. So do not be foolish, but understand what the will of the Lord is" (Ephesians 5:15–16, NRSV).

Called to Confidence and Freedom

Too often fear, inadequacy, or brokenness steal and destroy life, leaving the wounded paralyzed and lacking in confidence (John 10:10). When God calls you, our Lord will also provide the needed confidence for you to persevere and move ahead—even in spite of various hardships, setbacks, and frustrations.

God's Encouragement

Once when I was quite discouraged by personal circumstances, our family attended *The Christ Walk,* a moving drama depicting the life of Jesus. During the Last Supper scene, Jesus encouraged his disciples, "These things I have spoken to you, so that in me you may have peace. In the world you have tribulation, but take courage; I have over-come the world" (John 16:33, NASB).

With these words, Jesus so powerfully spoke to me and encouraged me that physically I felt his presence. Following this experience, daily I began to record how God appeared to me and encouraged me in the midst of ongoing discour-agement. Sometimes God's word filled me with courage. Sometimes it was an unexpected occurrence. Sometimes a friend or family member spoke an especially uplifting word. Sometimes I received surprise guidance or wisdom. In big and little epiphanies, God was living, active, and present, work-ing against my hurt, fear, insecurity, and discouragement.

I once observed a class taught by a friend. He later told me that my presence in the class caused him to feel more confident. Because this friend always seems quite confident, this comment surprised me. Being present in the class was really very simple. Just being there for someone can encour-age and support.

Encourage literally means to give inner courage. Ultimately, only our Lord can inspire inner courage and confidence, whether or not God uses a human being as an intermediary. God will build your confidence by encouraging and appear-ing to you.

Wholeness and Healing

Your confidence can be injured, diminished, and even destroyed by unhealed brokenness, prohibiting a life worthy of your call. Our Lord is the great physician and author of new beginnings.

Too often I can be quite a negative person. Through critical comments, I have inflicted my share of wounds. Slowly, I am learning that a simple, genuine, and positive comment can make all the difference, even healing hard and hurtful experiences from the past.

People readily become broken and burdened in countless ways. Your own sin can fracture your life. Deceit and careless words inflicted by another can leave you wounded. You may be injured by the unpredictable state of brokenness in the world created by a natural disaster, accident, tragedy, disease, or death.

Unhealed brokenness can undermine your confidence. Unhealed brokenness can trigger fear of what others think of you. It can produce hesitation. It can distract you. Unhealed brokenness can cause you to run from helpful feedback presented in a healthy manner. I am not talking about destructive feedback spoken with a harsh tone or as an attack. Unhealed and unresolved brokenness can be transferred from past relationships to present relationships of a similar nature. Then as result of feeling threatened, you will either attack or retreat inside. Even worse, brokenness can leave you paralyzed—unable to do anything.

God can graciously heal and transform you through many safe and non-threatening means: healing prayer, anointing with oil, laying-on of hands, encouragement, a medical doctor, a professional counselor, the passage of time, God's powerful Word, God's gentle whisper, worship, or other spiritual practices—to name just a few ways. Through oil upon my forehead and hands laid upon me, more than once God's Spirit has breathed new life into me.

You can press on and persevere through hard times by

reflecting upon God's promises. *Diminishing Difficulties with God's Precious Promises*, found in Appendix B, is a promise list assembled from my own powerful experience of meditating on scripture. God's Word can transform you.

Healing and wholeness can be unleashed through confession (James 5:16). Somehow the mere mention of confession often causes *fear*. Remember our God is not the author of fear. "Do not be afraid." In reality, confession is quite easy. Richard Foster offers simple instructions for a confession exercise particularly helpful to me. Divide your life into three periods: childhood, adolescence, and adulthood. On the first day, come before God in prayerful meditation. With paper and pencil in hand, invite God to reveal anything during your childhood that needs either forgiveness or healing or both. Then waiting in absolute silence for some minutes, allow God's gentle whisper to reveal what is needed. Record all that comes to mind without attempting to analyze any of it. On the following day, do this same exercise for your adolescence. In turn, do the same on a third day for your adult years. Then perhaps go to someone who understands confession. Confess and share your thoughts. You will need to confess to someone who is non-judgmental and utterly safe on confidentiality, perhaps someone you do not know.[1]

Once in the midst of this exercise, God whispered to me, "I want you to cry." At the time, this message puzzled me. Over the next couple of weeks, from time to time one of those painful incidents would interrupt my thoughts. Suddenly without warning, I would break into tears, sometimes even weeping. Don't worry! I was not in front of an audience; instead, nearly always I was by myself. After those couple of weeks, a measure of wholeness was present that previously was absent.

Our Lord is calling you to true freedom (Galatians 5:1, 13). Confession will set you free from bondage, even if years have passed since an offense. Simply seeking the wounded one and specifically acknowledging your wrongs while requesting forgiveness can set both of you free. I have heard story after story of great healing. A divorced friend confessed her wrongs first in a letter and later in a conversation with her former spouse, freeing her from guilt and regret. Confession can set loose cleansing. Perhaps best of all, confession can free you from your past, so you can move ahead unencumbered into the future.

Compensating for Your Weaknesses

Owning our weaknesses can be difficult. Ironically, acknowledging our weaknesses and then compensating for them leads to profound strength and confidence. Recognizing your need for others' unique gifts and characteristics to supplement and complement your own will increase your effectiveness. In the midst of weakness, you will even experience God's great power (2 Corinthians 12:7–10).

Acquiring Needed Experience and Training

The destination sometimes may seem so slow in coming.

For many years, God has been calling me to write these pages while simultaneously preparing and training me to do the same. God set in motion my custom designed preparation plan a very long time ago. Countless out of the community of faith have contributed—mentors, teachers, professors, authors, seminar leaders, pastors, preachers and my parents. For years, many have molded and made my belief. Seeking and searching, I have learned about life with my living Lord Jesus. Mentors taught me to mine the amazing message of God's word, not to mention listening and leaning on my Lord. The still small voice of the Spirit surfaced in silence and solitude. How rich it has been! Then my teaching gift transpired as I gained effectiveness and experience. Practical insights and skills supplemented my gifts—like leading a discussion and designing a class. Adding ancient insights with tried and true traditions has enriched my exploration and experience. Comprehending complex theological concepts has added depth and dimension. Meanwhile, many minds and hearts have heard the message of God's constant and compelling call. Without trying, I have trained others to teach about God's call. Not coincidentally, I have cultivated my writing skills all along. One of my pastoral mentors used to say that it is tough to traverse with others where you have not already adventured yourself. Personal experience is apt preparation.

Simply put, I cannot be a car mechanic unless I have some knowledge about how to fix a car. Through learning, experimentation, prior experience, or seeking help from a skilled mechanic, I can attempt to fix a car. At a minimum, I need to have a process for examining a car, troubleshooting, and then making needed adjustments.

God has a preparation plan for you. God will train and equip you with needed insights and abilities, increasing your confidence and freeing you from fear. Likewise, God has custom designed a destination for you. What is behind will prepare for what is ahead. God's call is dynamic. Tomorrow's call will be different from today. Training and teaching, along with confidence and courage will be your companions.

"For this reason I remind you to rekindle the gift of God that is within you through the laying on of my hands; for God did not give us a spirit of fear, but rather a spirit of power and of love and of self-discipline" (2 Timothy 1:6–7, NRSV).

Custom Designing a Life Worthy of the Call

Custom designed and custom called for a custom designed life! What would a fruitful and abundant life look like for you? How could you live a life worthy of your call? What is needed? A custom designed life is possible.

Throughout history, individuals, families, churches and other groups of Christians have created patterns of life. Monastic communities like the Benedictines or Franciscans have established a rule of life. For them, a rule meant a measure or pattern. These patterns integrated such things as manual work, prayer, and principles for relationships and lifestyle. Even now, people who live in houses rather than monasteries employ these wise rules to pattern their lives.

With God's guidance, you can custom design your own

pattern, creating a blueprint or plan for building your life. Establishing a pattern of life will be very valuable for intentionally incorporating and integrating needed and helpful steps into the rhythm of your life. A well-designed pattern of life will assist in developing a relationship of depth with Jesus, helping you to *know, follow,* and *uniquely serve* him.

To stimulate your thinking, specific examples are provided. They are not for you to imitate or emulate. Resist the temptation to copy or compare yourself to these samples. Since your lifestyle is unique, your pattern will also be custom designed. As in the first example, a part of your pattern may be left blank for future practice, growth, and change.

A Pattern of Life: First Example

Call to Know Jesus
- I will spend five minutes with God in the evening. I will experiment with reflecting upon a verse or two of Scripture.
- Until I find a church that fits me, I will worship at two different churches each month.

Call to Follow Jesus

Call to Uniquely Serve Jesus
- When I travel on an airplane, I will set aside an hour to work on one of the steps in this book.
- In the next six months, I will attend a class on spiritual gifts.
- Twice a month on Friday night, I will have a date with my spouse.

- At my job, I will consider what is energizing and fulfilling to me and what is not. I will invite God to give me wisdom in my work.
- In my spaces of time, I will reflect upon the financial principles in this book, considering how I can make needed changes.

Instructions and Guidelines

A pattern of life is designed best in the context of quiet, careful, and prayerful reflection. Invite God to guide you. To assist you in creating and recording your pattern of life, a worksheet is provided in Appendix C. What do you need to live according to your call? Reflect upon the many ideas throughout this entire volume. As you contemplate this season of your life, select a few helpful exercises. Be realistic, choosing ideas that are attainable. Think about steps suggested by others as well. Seek counsel from those with great wisdom and experience—perhaps your pastor, priest, spiritual director, or a trustworthy friend. Choose practices *freely* desired by you rather than those you feel obligated to do. For now, ignore those steps that are uncomfortable.

If creating a pattern of life is new to you, begin by using the worksheet to evaluate your present lifestyle. Finally, employ the worksheet a second time, drafting your intentions for the future. Design your pattern to fit your unique circumstances. Record when, how often, where, and how you will accomplish the various practices. Narrative form is not necessary. A few words will suffice. Make your pattern simple and specific. Volume is not the goal. Make your pattern flexible. Ensure that it feels comfortable for this point in your life. Remember your pattern should fit your unique lifestyle. Regularly reflect upon your pattern, adapting it as needed—perhaps every six months to a year or more often. If it is not working or becomes irrelevant, identify what is not working, and make needed changes. Your pattern should evolve over time, reflecting both changes in your lifestyle and your unique call.

A Pattern of Life: Second Example

Call to Know Jesus
- I will worship weekly, hearing God's Word and celebrating the Lord's Supper. I will write down in a notebook one new insight that I learned as a result of hearing God's Word.
- Daily with my first available time, I will spend fifteen minutes with God. I will begin by resting in God's love. I will pray the letter that I wrote to God. I will use a devotional from church for the remainder of the time.
- I will walk in the early evening on Tuesday and Friday evening. While I walk, I will pay attention to my thoughts.

Call to Follow Jesus
- Once a month, I will set aside a Saturday morning for intentional time with God. The first time, I will write a letter to God. As a part of this letter, I will invite the Holy Spirit to continually fill

me. After this initial time, I will use this time for solitude and meditation.

- Once a month I will arrange to have an intentional conversation with one of my trusted friends. Before meeting, I will pray about what I might like to share with them.

Call to Uniquely Serve Jesus

- Over the next six months, I will evaluate how I am presently serving in my church gathering. I will explore new opportunities that may be more fulfilling to me using my shepherding and intercession spiritual gifts.
- On Sunday afternoon, I will spend one half hour reflecting upon my uniqueness and how I might better use my spiritual gifts.
- Weekly, I will look for new ways to give of my resources.
- On Sunday afternoons once a month, I will spend one hour working on my heartfelt desires and lifelong goals for my work, family and home, church, neighborhood, community, and world.
- On my commute over the next three months, I will consider why I am restless at work.

Your pattern will create health and wholeness. Best of all, you will come to know and experience the immense love of your greatest friend Jesus, in an immeasurable way. You have a custom designed life—find it and live it!

"Now to him who is able to do far more abundantly beyond all that we [continually] ask or think, according to the power that [continually] works within us, to him be the glory in the church [called-out-ones] and in Christ Jesus to all generations forever and ever. Amen. Therefore I, the prisoner of the Lord, implore [earnestly call] you to walk in a manner worthy of the calling with which you have been called" (Ephesians 3:20–4:1, NASB) (Author's translation in brackets).

The Called-out Ones: Working Together

Custom Designing a Church or Organization around God's Call

Organization is akin to organism; therefore, an organization is alive.

God's plans almost always have been accomplished through people. Remember you are the church. We are the church together. Therefore, the church is also alive. For years, my husband and I have worked with church gatherings, custom designing around the unique calls of people. Businesses and other organizations have implemented these same "call" principles.

If custom designing is done well, an organization will work together more effectively. The scope of its efforts will grow. The level of satisfaction within it will increase.

Because every person is unique, custom designing an

organization around the individual "calls" of people also will be very unique. Mind you, this is not a program as if God can be reduced to a program, a simple step one, step two, and step three. An organization can custom design its structure and even its future direction by seeking to know the unique calls of people. In pursuing this approach, an organization might need to lay aside any preconceived notions for its structure, plans, and direction. A schematic for custom designing around "call" is shown in Diagram D. Please note that for most churches or organizations, the arrows will point in the opposite direction from those shown on the diagram.

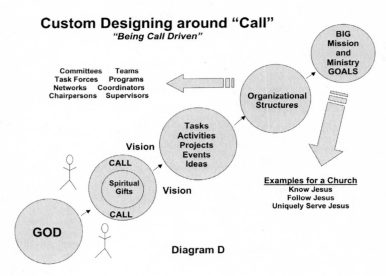

Custom Designing around "Call"
"Being Call Driven"

BIG Mission and Ministry GOALS

Committees   Teams
Task Forces   Programs
Networks   Coordinators
Chairpersons Supervisors

Organizational Structures

Tasks
Activities
Projects
Events
Ideas

Vision

CALL

Spiritual Gifts

Vision

CALL

GOD

Examples for a Church
Know Jesus
Follow Jesus
Uniquely Serve Jesus

Diagram D

To some degree, these principles may be implemented in all settings: the church, Christian organizations, Christian businesses, other organizations and businesses. In fact, the church is supposed to function in this way (1 Corinthians 12, Romans

12). Therefore, church gatherings and other Christian organizations can apply these principles to a great degree.

Depending upon your daily setting, these principles will be utilized differently. To begin, you must evaluate whether you have a position of influence. If not, unless those in leadership roles are interested in employing this approach, investing your time will be pointless. In turn, if your group is not Christian, then the language describing these principles may differ out of respect for those who are not Christian.

Continuum of Implementation

Each place on this continuum represents a greater degree of building around the calls of people. As you consider this continuum, you must decide the place that is workable and comfortable for you.

- *Individual:* Live a life worthy of your call. You can seek to know how God has created and custom designed you. In turn, you can listen for God's call, living it in the arenas and roles of life where God has placed you.
- *Individual:* In addition to the above, you can encourage others to understand their custom design and call. This alone will enrich your group. Having a call conversation is a helpful skill for you to learn.
- *Leader:* In addition to the above, assuming that you have a supervisory or coordinating role, you can complete tasks and fill pre-designed slots by seeking to know the best person for them. Based upon their unique attributes and desire to work on certain activities, you can fill needed roles with the

people who best fit them. You even may modify and custom design various tasks and roles around the individuals who will function in them.

- *Leader:* In addition to the above, you can create an organizational structure that maximizes people's gifts and strengths, and still allows for needed accountability. Custom designing an organizational structure will create a productive team while minimizing the time spent in meetings and troubleshooting.
- *Leader:* In addition to the above, you can design the direction of a group around the calls of individuals. This will promote creative energy, innovative initiatives, fresh ideas, and promising direction.

In order to implement this approach effectively, leaders will require more skills and greater knowledge at each spot on the continuum. The needed skills and knowledge are the scope of another book.

God desires that people should work together, effectively accomplishing their common work, goals, and purposes. Because every individual is custom designed, each has a unique function that will promote the group's growth and development. Imagine the transformational power of God's people as these truths are discovered and lived out!

———————

"We must grow up in every way into him who is the head, into Christ, from whom the whole body, joined and knit together by every ligament with which it is equipped, as each part is working properly, the body's growth is promoted, building itself up in love" (Ephesians 4:15b-16, NIV).

Appendix A

Talents, Skills, and Abilities

Performing Skills

___ Public Speaking	___ Dramatics: Speaking/Reading	___ Pantomime	___ Puppeteer	___ Leading Games
___ Presentations	___ Skits/Plays	___ Dance	___ Choir	___ Sing solos/duets
___ Comedy	___ Handbells	___ Play Instrument	___ Small Group Singing	___ Spontaneity
___ Compose Music	___ Preaching	___ Interpreting for the deaf	___ Lecturing	Other: Specify

Artistic and Other Creative Skills

___ Drawing	___ Scrapbooks	___ Designing	___ Posters/ Charts	___ Adult Crafts
___ Painting	___ Knitting	___ Photography	___ Interior Design	___ Creating or Innovating

___ Woodworking	___ Sewing	___ Graphic Arts	___ Decorating	___ Stitching
___ Displays	___ Weaving or Banners	___ Making Videos	___ Child Crafts	Other: Specif

Practical Skills

___ Masonry	___ Electrical Skills	___ Mechanical	___ Plumbing	___ Small Engine Repai
___ Maintenance	___ Carpentry	___ Gardening	___ Cleaning	___ Data Bas Management
___ Landscaping	___ Painting	___ Heating/ AC	___ Organize Meals	___ Web Page Management
___ Cabinet Making	___ Wallpapering	___ Inventing	___ Cook in Large Quantities	___ Handyperson
___ Lawn Mowing	___ Trimming	___ Computer Skills	___ Construction	Other: Specif

Administrative Skills

___ Data Entry	___ Editing/ Proofing	___ Run Meetings	___ Set Priorities	___ Reporting
___ Telephoning	___ Budgeting	___ Making Policy	___ Supervising	___ Record Keeping
___ Library Skills	___ Administrating	___ Coordinating	___ General Office	___ Financial
___ Filing	___ Planning	___ Organization	___ Receptionist	___ Bookkeeping

Writing Skills

___ Informational or Newsletter Articles	___ Devotions	___ Essays/ Stories	___ Drama	___ Poetry

Outreach Skills

___ Marketing or Promoting	___ Human Relations	___ Cultural Trends	___ Research or Demographics	___ Foreign Languages

People Skills

___ Welcoming	___ Teaching	___ Team Building	___ Recruiting	___ Mediating
___ Talking with Strangers & Visitors	___ Tutoring	___ Motivating or Inspiring	___ Working with Groups	___ Solving Conflicts
___ Listening	___ Training	___ Speak a Foreign Language	___ Trouble Shooting	___ Other: Specify

Appendix B

Diminishing Difficulties with
God's Powerful Promises

The Ds: Difficulties

Darkness ... Disappointment ... Disillusionment ... Distraction ... Distress ... Despair ... Driven ... Doubt ... Danger ... Depression ... Discouragement ... Destruction ... Death

Replacing the Ds with the Ps—God's Powerful Promises

Difficulties do not go away. However, God's *powerful promises* will speak to you, sustaining you in the midst of the difficulties.

Pressing On ... Philippians 3:7–14
Perseverance ... Hebrews 12:1–3

Perspective ... Romans 8:35–39

Play and Rest ... Matthew 11:28–30

Prayer is a Conversation with God ... Philippians 4:6–7

Possibility ... Luke 1:37

Present Moment ... Philippians 3:13, Matthew 6:34

Presence of God (all the time) ... Matthew 28:20, Hebrews 13:5–6

Peace ... Wholeness ... John 14:25–27, Philippians 4:8–9

Patience ... Isaiah 40:30–31

Positives ... 1 Peter 4:8

Partners ... James 5:13–16

Preparation and Training ... 1 Timothy 4:7–8

Practice ... Matthew 7:24–27

Priorities ... Matthew 6:33

Plan of God ... Jeremiah 29:11–14

Purpose ... 1 Corinthians 2:9

Power ... 2 Corinthians 12:9, Ephesians 3:20

Praise ... Ephesians 1:9

Pattern for Living ... Ephesians 4:1

Appendix C

Pattern of Life Worksheet

Call to Know Jesus

How will you deepen and grow your friendship with Jesus?

Describe practices that you would like to do. Be specific about how and when you will do these practices. Use words and phrases that will be easily remembered.

Call to Follow Jesus

How will you seek Jesus' guidance, freedom, and grace and seek to follow him in all of life?

Describe practices that you would like to do. Be specific about how and when you will do these practices. Again use words and phrases.

- *Listening for God's voice:*
- *Learning:*
- *Letting Go:*

Call to Serve Jesus

How will you seek to serve Jesus in the arenas of life listed below?

Describe opportunities, responsibilities, and practices that you might like to do. Be specific. Consider the following:

- Use of your time
- Use of your spiritual gifts, talents, skills, knowledge, experience
- Use of your money, home, other material goods, and property
- Witness: Sharing your faith story and experience of Jesus with others

Family and Friends
Work (career, paid or volunteer, at home)
Body of Christ... People of God... Church
Community/Neighborhood/World

Obstacles? What do you need to learn (spiritual, practical, relationships, intellectual)? What training do you need? How and when could you do this learning?

Who could help you if you need some feedback or guidance? Who do you trust to give you this kind of feedback or guidance?

Bibliography

Books

Bolles, Richard Nelson. *A Practical Manual for Job Hunters & Career-Changers: The 1993 What Color Is Your Parachute.* Berkeley, CA: Ten Speed Press, 1993.

Buford, Bob. *Halftime Changing Your Game Plan from Success to Significance.* Grand Rapids, MI: Zondervan, 1994.

Foster, Richard. *Celebration of Discipline the Path to Spiritual Growth.* New York: Harper & Row, Publishers Inc., 1978.

Foster, Richard. *Prayer Finding the Heart's True Home.* New York: HarperCollins, 1992.

Inter-Lutheran Commission on Worship (Lutheran Church in America, The American Lutheran Church, The Evangelical Lutheran Church of Canada, The Lutheran Church—Missouri Synod). *Lutheran Book of*

Worship. Minneapolis: Augsburg Publishing House and Philadelphia: Board of Publications, Lutheran Church in America, 1978.

Lawrence, Brother. *The Practice of the Presence of God.* Old Tappan, NJ: Revell, 1958.

Parton, Dolly. *Coat of Many Colors.* New York: HarperCollins, 1994.

Videos

Hybels, Bill. *Imagine a Church* video from *NETWORK The Right People ... In the Right Places ... For the Right Reasons.* Grand Rapids, MI: Zondervan, 1994.

Conferences

Vaswig, William. July 3, 1999 address at *"The Divine Conspiracy: A Renovare International Conference on Spiritual Renewal."* Houston, TX.

Endnotes

Called to be Gifted and Empowered

1. Bill Hybels, *Imagine a Church* video from *NETWORK The Right People...In the Right Places...For the Right Reasons.* Grand Rapids, MI: Zondervan, 1994.

Called to the Greatest Relationship

1. Richard Nelson Bolles, *A Practical Manual for Job Hunters & Career-Changers: The 1993 What Color Is Your Parachute.* Berkeley, CA: Ten Speed Press, 1993, p. 364.

2. Bob Buford, *Half Time Changing Your Game Plan from Success to Significance.* Grand Rapids, MI: Zondervan, 1994, pp. 62–66.

Called to Inspiration

1. Brother Lawrence, *The Practice of the Presence of God.* Old Tappan, NJ: Revell, 1958, p. 9.

Called to the Great Reversal

1. Richard Foster, *Prayer Finding the Heart's True Home.* New York: HarperCollins, 1992, p. 123.
2. William Vaswig, July 3, 1999 address at *"The Divine Conspiracy: A Renovare International Conference on Spiritual Renewal."* Houston, TX.

Called to a Wise Economy of Life

1. Inter-Lutheran Commission on Worship (Lutheran Church in America, The American Lutheran Church, The Evangelical Lutheran Church of Canada, The Lutheran Church–Missouri Synod), *Lutheran Book of Worship.* Minneapolis: Augsburg Publishing House and Philadelphia: Board of Publications, Lutheran Church in America, 1978, p. 67.
2. Dolly Parton, *Coat of Many Colors.* New York: HarperCollins, 1994.

Called to Confidence and Freedom

1. Richard Foster, *Celebration of Discipline the Path to Spiritual Growth.* New York: Harper & Row, Publishers Inc., 1978, p. 131.

e|LIVE

listen|imagine|view|experience

AUDIO BOOK DOWNLOAD INCLUDED WITH THIS BOOK!

In your hands you hold a complete digital entertainment package. Besides purchasing the paper version of this book, this book includes a free download of the audio version of this book. Simply use the code listed below when visiting our website. Once downloaded to your computer, you can listen to the book through your computer's speakers, burn it to an audio CD or save the file to your portable music device (such as Apple's popular iPod) and listen on the go!

How to get your free audio book digital download:

1. Visit www.tatepublishing.com and click on the e|LIVE logo on the home page.
2. Enter the following coupon code:
   e09f-5ad1-1df9-8862-7eef-f5f1-be00-121f
3. Download the audio book from your e|LIVE digital locker and begin enjoying your new digital entertainment package today!